Salvation Theology

AN INTRODUCTION *to* SOTERIOLOGY

Salvation Theology

AN INTRODUCTION *to* SOTERIOLOGY

JOSEPH THOMAS

 Scepter

Salvation Theology: An Introduction to Soteriology © 2021 Joseph Thomas.

Also copyright © 2021 Scepter Publishers, Inc.

Published by Scepter Publishers, Inc.
info@scepterpublishers.org
www.scepterpublishers.org
800-322-8773
New York

Cover design by StudioRed Designs
Page design and pagination by Rose Design

Library of Congress Control Number: 2021934295

ISBN: 9781594174209 (pbk.)
ISBN: 9781594174216 (eBook)

Printed in the United States of America

CONTENTS

INTRODUCTION

~~~

What exactly is salvation? What does it mean to be "saved"? This work seeks to offer a theological response to these questions.

The area of theology which examines these questions is known as *soteriology*. The word comes from the Greek term *soter*, which means "savior." In the ancient world, this word had a variety of meanings. It could indicate the pagan gods who were thought to save people from danger. *Soter* would also signify a human being who literally saves a life, such as a physician. The term was also used to describe a ruler, in particular the Roman emperor, who was worshipped as a god.

With the Incarnation of the Son of God, a *Savior* has appeared in the fullest sense. This book seeks to describe the saving action of Christ. After analyzing the concepts of *salvation* and *redemption*, we will examine the way God has carried out these actions through the *mediation* of Christ. This mediation brings to fulfillment the roles of priest, prophet, and king found in the Old Testament.

Afterwards, we will look at how Christ lives this mediation through each moment of his life: his coming in the flesh, his ordinary work, his public ministry, and especially his passion, death, and resurrection. In all of these circumstances, Christ saves us from sin and manifests the divine meaning of human life.

Finally, we will analyze how Christ's salvific mediation continues after his ascension. By the gift of the Holy Spirit, Christians experience the fruits of salvation here and now, at the same time as they look forward to the fullness of salvation at Christ's second coming.

In all of these topics, the Christian faith offers penetrating answers to the questions that Christians and others might have about salvation and redemption. However, the study of soteriology is never simply a question of satisfying intellectual curiosity. Our inquiry is an important way of responding to the Church's continued insistence that the mystery of Jesus Christ be ever more at the center of the Christian's thoughts, words, and deeds.

In this work, I am thankful for being able to draw from a large number of sources, which form part of the Church's rich and centuries-old theological reflection. These fonts are mentioned at the end of the book and can serve as resources for further study.

CHAPTER 1

Salvation: A Human Desire and Divine Gift

Human beings experience the finite but hope for the infinite. Though conscious of life's brevity, we do not cease working, struggling, and searching for happiness. Our effort is aimed at the future; it points toward something we can fully realize, something total, something more than the passing experience of earthly happiness.

—Jutta Burggraf, German theologian, 1952–2010

A. Human Aspiration to Salvation, Constant in All History

Salvation is not an easy concept to define. Nevertheless, God's revelation gives constant testament to this truth. From beginning to end, Scripture bears witness to the reality that the human being needs to be saved. God has willed to respond to this necessity, and has done so in a definitive manner in Jesus Christ. At the moment of his conception, an angel announces to Joseph that Christ "will save his people from their sins" (Mt 1:21).

Despite these evident scriptural truths, the fact of "needing to be saved" might not strike us as something immediately evident. As we know, human society has taken many steps forward in recent years. Science, technology, and health care have achieved unprecedented levels of development. The decline of religious practice in numerous countries makes concepts such as salvation and redemption less and less understandable to many people.

Still, when we scratch the surface, we can detect, also by reason, the deep wounds which have been left in us and society as a result of sin. Vatican II's Constitution on the Church in the Modern World, *Gaudium et Spes*, expresses a great appreciation for the advances of human civilization in modern times. But it also notes that "what divine revelation makes known to us agrees with experience. Examining his heart, man finds that he has inclinations toward evil too, and is engulfed by manifold ills which cannot come from his good Creator."

The continuation and proliferation of horrific acts of violence, the repression and injustice that countless persons face, the prevalence of harmful addictions of various types, among other troubling phenomena, point toward a larger affliction that affects the human race as a whole. As much as human beings might like to deny or ignore it, the human race—and each human being—stands in urgent need of the salvation which only the Creator can offer.

Pointing out such problems in individuals or societies is not a matter of being negative or pessimistic. In order to better appreciate the meaning of salvation, we need to realize that we are in need of redemption. Men and women have a deep desire for deliverance from the sinful condition that affects human nature.

St. Josemaría Escrivá, commenting on the gospel, liked to consider the multitudes of persons today who, despite appearances to the contrary, are thirsting for God and his revelation:

> Can't you see? They want to hear God's message, even though outwardly they may not show it. Some perhaps have forgotten Christ's teachings. Others, through no fault of their own, have never known them and they think that religion is something odd.

Still, even in these conditions of apparent indifference to God, the founder of Opus Dei asserted that we can recognize the emptiness present in our lives due to the absence of God:

> But of this we can be sure, that in every man's life there comes a time sooner or later when his soul draws the line. He has had enough of the usual explanations. The lies of the false prophets no longer satisfy. Even though they may not admit it at the time, such people are longing to quench their thirst with the teachings of Our Lord.

The Bible is a privileged witness to our need to be rescued and redeemed from our fallen condition. Shortly after the Creation accounts, the sacred author of Genesis states that "the earth was corrupt in God's sight, and the earth was filled with violence," to the point that God intends to destroy the human race (Gn 6:11). The righteous anger of God at the immorality of human beings is the initial topic of St. Paul's Letter to the Romans, the great epistle which describes the salvation brought about through Christ. The apostle speaks of the wrath of God, directed against "all ungodliness and wickedness of men who by their wickedness suppress the truth" (Rom 1:18). The sinful tendency behind such wickedness does not belong to a select group of so-called "evil" people; it is a danger against which all must be on guard (see Rom 2:1).

Inspired by this biblical perspective and his knowledge of the pagan world, St. Athanasius of Alexandria—the fourth-century bishop in Egypt and stalwart defender of Christ's identity—describes in vivid detail the depraved condition of the human race:

> For even in their misdeeds men had not stopped short at any set limits . . . having turned aside to wrong and exceeding all lawlessness, and stopping at no one evil but devising all manner of new evils in succession, they have become insatiable in

sinning. For there were adulteries everywhere and thefts, and the whole earth was full of murders and plunderings." This great champion of the Christian faith realized that an awareness of the sinful situation of man was important to accurately describe the work of salvation carried out by Christ.

Certainly, the special grace of faith allowed the above writers to appreciate the truth of our need for salvation. Still, we should not think of this truth as exclusive to believers. In different ways, the development of the great religions shows our desire to transcend the world around us. Ancient Chinese culture and its great teacher, Confucius, had a vivid awareness that the source of human vitality relied on a wisdom that comes from heaven. The writers of the Upanishads, a set of sacred books revered in Hinduism, sought to reach beyond the created universe to grasp the Absolute.

In this process, these non-Christian religions sought deliverance from the limitations of the human condition. The desire for "salvation" from the present world finds a particularly strong expression in Buddhism. While taking a less philosophical approach than the Hindu sacred texts, Buddhists look for deliverance and salvation from all human desire and thus from all suffering. Greek culture, as the twentieth-century British historian Christopher Dawson pointed out, follows a similar pattern. While it is not exactly clear what the Greeks held to be the nature of the gods, they recognized the existence of a divine order that human beings needed to obey through religious sacrifice and ritual.

Undoubtedly, the above religious views include visions of the universe and of salvation which are quite different from the biblical one. Still, these perspectives manifest a genuine *human desire for salvation* which is present across cultures. This desire, as the German theologian Jutta Burggraf noted, is essential to the human person: "By the fact of being an image of the infinite God, man holds in his heart an irrepressible need for the absolute and infinite." This desire, she further notes, points to the existence of an "absolute reality," God, who can correspond to this longing.

We recognize our limited and deficient condition, and try to reach beyond the limitations of this life and this world. We long to be rescued, saved, and led to a greater and fuller life.

Such a yearning for salvation can take various forms. In the first place, we look for a solution to the inescapable reality of death. Our life, as we know, is marked by awareness of the gradual decay of our bodies and our eventual death. While this process of decay affects all living creatures in the material world, in the human person the reality of death appears as a particular contradiction. Along with a natural desire for life to continue, we possess the unique capacity to recognize the fact of our mortality.

The very ability to know our own mortality implies that we have a certain capacity to transcend the material world. As creatures with a spiritual soul, we long for a happiness which is infinite, and as a result death appears to us as a contradiction of who we are. Such a dilemma has always deeply affected persons and continues to be a pressing one for many persons today. As the character in an acclaimed contemporary novel points out, "The deepest regret is death. The only thing to face is death. This is all I think about. . . . I want to live."

Along with death, human beings experience a set of other evils which go against our natural desires and the full development of our capacities. Such evils are known as *physical* evils and can include suffering in its various forms as well as poverty, injustice, and mental ills such as depression and excessive anxiety. In addition, we experience in ourselves and around us the sad reality of *moral evil*, in which we knowingly reject the moral law. In part, this evil is due to a tendency to sin, known as concupiscence, which is present in each person. We find that we are unable to fulfill the moral law to which our conscience gives testimony, and at times we freely choose against this law. Finally, there is *metaphysical evil*, which refers to the natural limitations of any creature. We recognize that, on our own, we cannot attain the fullness of happiness and life that we long for.

In the case of many people around us, the awareness of such contradictions sadly leads them to turn away from God. Some seek consolation in purely earthly ambitions which appear to offer them "salvation." Others fall into despair and lose the very drive to live. Still, it is precisely the experience of such limitations that can form a starting point for understanding the reality of salvation.

B. Salvation: Initiative of the God of the Covenant

The Church seeks to speak to us in the experience of such limits and uncertainties. She recognizes, as the Constitution *Gaudium et Spes* noted, that

> in the face of the modern development of the world, the num-
> ber constantly swells of the people who raise the most basic
> questions or recognize them with a new sharpness: what is man?
> What is this sense of sorrow, of evil, of death, which continues
> to exist despite so much progress? What purpose have these vic-
> tories purchased at so high a cost? What can man offer to soci-
> ety, what can he expect from it? What follows this earthly life?

Christians recognize and are concerned for these problems which afflict the human condition, but also realize that the distress and sorrow present in human life have a deeper root. The evils in the world are not primarily the result of material defi-
ciencies, but of a disorder present in the human heart: our deci-
sion to turn away from God by *sin*. As the Congregation for the Doctrine of the Faith has stated,

> It is this separation from God—He who is the fount of com-
> munion and life—that brings about the loss of harmony

among human persons, and between humanity and the world, introducing the dominion of disintegration and death (see Rom 5:12).

The response of the Church to this sad situation is not simply a theory, nor is it merely a psychological consolation to distress. The Church offers *salvation*. As the Second Vatican Council affirmed in *Gaudium et Spes*,

> The Church firmly believes that Christ, who died and was raised up for all, can through His Spirit offer man the light and the strength to measure up to his supreme destiny. Nor has any other name under heaven been given to man by which it is fitting for him to be saved.

God bestows his own divine life on us through the Holy Spirit. He gives "light" to the intellect and "strength" to the will, and only in this way can each person's deepest desires be brought to fulfillment.

This salvation can only come from the initiative of God, who comes to the aid of our limitations and weaknesses. Salvation is also ultimately oriented toward God, as we find our true fulfillment in the participation in God's own life. At the same time, in order to lead us to this divine end, God speaks to us in light of our own experience. If the limitations of the human being without God show us the need for salvation, we can say that salvation consists precisely in God's offer of himself to enter into dialogue with us.

God makes a *covenant* with his people, implicitly with Adam and explicitly with Noah, Abraham, and Moses. Through this covenant, he commits himself to his people while in return demanding their faithfulness. The pages of the Old Testament give witness to God's initiative to start this conversation, beginning with creation. He continues this dialogue despite original sin and gradually leads his people toward the full expression of himself realized in the definitive Word of God, Jesus Christ.

From this perspective, we can appreciate how salvation reaches beyond this world but at the same time has a concrete manifestation in history. Words derived from the Hebrew root *yasha*, which is used in the words *salvation* and *to save*, occur more than three hundred times in the Old Testament. Scripture uses such words with various shades of meaning, but they all relate to a "fundamental experience," as the French Scripture scholars Colomban Lesquivit and Pierre Grelot point out: "To be saved is to be taken out of a dangerous situation in which one risked perishing."

In the Old Testament, such saving action takes on very concrete forms, such as protection and liberation from enemies, ransom from slavery, bodily health and life, military victory, and peace. God saves the life of Lot from the punishment of the wicked, at the intercession of Moses (see Gn 18:22; Wis 10:6). By means of David and other leaders of Israel, God saves his people from the power of their enemies (see 2 Sm 3:18). While this salvation has a concrete material aspect, it also remains connected with the moral good which God desires for the Chosen People. In the Old Testament, God always accompanies his saving action with a judgment, in which the just are set apart from the sinners.

These more tangible experiences of salvation formed the basis for understanding the deeper liberation which God would bring about in the soul of the person by means of sanctifying grace. The saving power of God is shown in a literal way through countless actions of military victory and liberation, and especially in the miraculous escape of the Chosen People from slavery in Egypt. Through this experience, the People of God come to know the truth revealed to the prophet Isaiah: "I, I am the LORD, and besides me there is no savior." (Is 43:11).

Over the course of the Old Testament, the saving power of God toward his people came to be understood more clearly in terms of the *kingdom* which he desired to establish. At the request of his people and by means of the prophet Samuel, God appoints a king who stands for the authority and sovereignty which belong to God alone. David's kingship served as a "golden age" which Israel would later look back on, in which God gave his people victory over their enemies.

In the face of their later tribulations, the People of God also looked forward to a future messiah who would bring God's definitive salvation. The long-expected messiah would bring a long-awaited security, victory, and peace. This concept of salvation, held by the Jews in the centuries before Christ, had a mix of material and spiritual elements. In the Jewish view, the salvation brought by the messiah was not wholly focused on eternal life but included the expectation of an earthly kingdom. The Chosen People longed for the safety and security which God promised to give them in their own land. At the same time, they also awaited "a new heart" and "a new spirit" through which Israel would be interiorly purified (Ez 36:26).

C. Christ, Universal Savior

"But when the time had fully come, God sent forth his Son, born of woman, born under the law, to redeem those who were under the law, so that we might receive adoption as sons" (Gal 4:4–5). With the Incarnation of the Second Person of the Trinity, God offers the salvation—in the fullest sense of the term—which he has in mind for the human race. As St. Paul tells us, this salvation is not a liberation from physical ills or servitude but from the "law." This law, as the apostle indicates in the Letter to the Romans, manifests to us the reality of sin and can even serve as a temptation toward sin (see 7:7–10).

Certainly, Christ responds to the human desire for material liberation through his healings and other miracles. Still, the

New Testament makes it clear that Christ has come to save us from the most perilous danger which faces us: sin. With the grace offered through Christ, and poured into us by the Holy Spirit, God gives us the strength to overcome sinfulness and our inability to follow the moral law on our own.

In this way, God carries out the work of salvation in the *heart* of each person. However, this should not lead us to think of salvation as something exclusively "interior" or even simply "otherworldly." Many people today ask, "Are you saved?" Behind this question there can be a vision of salvation, common today, which is—as the Congregation for the Doctrine of the Faith observes—"marked by a strong personal conviction or feeling of being united to God." Some people, taking this idea to an extreme, think that salvation would be a "liberation," by which we would be elevated into an otherworldly realm. In this view, salvation would mean an escape from the body and the material universe.

Such convictions might be genuine and have some noble aspects. Still, salvation cannot be reduced to a sense of personal certainty on the part of the individual, because it is a gift which no human effort can attain. Moreover, salvation, when accepted in faith in the human heart, transforms the entire human condition. It affects us in body and soul, and in our relationships with others. Through the gift of salvation, God desires to heal and renew the entire created world.

As the New Testament makes clear, salvation is offered to the Chosen People but also to all persons: "He who believes and is baptized will be saved; but he who does not believe will be condemned" (Mk 16:16). In these and many other passages of the New Testament, God's revelation gives witness to Christ's role as the one Savior for all humanity.

The early Church sought to present Christ not simply as the fulfillment of Israel's longing for salvation but also as the answer to the desires for truth and goodness found among all humanity.

St. Justin Martyr, the great second-century Christian thinker, argued that not just Hebrew Scriptures but also pagan culture pointed to Christ. Pagan religion and philosophy, according to Justin, contains veiled messages of the Holy Spirit which indicate the true Savior, Jesus.

The Fathers of the Church argued that Christ is the fullness of the knowledge which the Gnostics—a sect in the early centuries of Christianity—sought in their heretical ideas. The Fathers further asserted that Jesus is not simply the source of salvation in a spiritual sense. Christ, they held, also offers the promise of an earthly liberation: from oppression, disease, poverty, and mortality.

The salvation offered in Christ, while being supernatural, responds in particular to one of the deepest longings which humans have: *peace*. In a sense, the concept of peace contains within itself all of the benefits of salvation. Many persons today, with or without faith, earnestly desire this good. Nonetheless, they recognize that despite their best efforts, true peace remains elusive. Christ, whom St. Paul describes as "our peace" (Eph 2:14), has come to fulfill this deep human desire. He offers a peace which is not simply the absence of conflict but also the fruit of a proper ordering of humanity in our relationship to God and others. It is a peace which requires the virtues of justice and charity.

The goodness and truth found in the various world religions have led some to consider that each religion might have its own path of salvation. Some theologians and others see Christ as a particular historical figure who is not the exclusive path to God. Rather, Christ is just one among other "salvific figures." Some have proposed what they call an "economy of the Holy Spirit," which would work in a more universal way than the "economy of Christ." In such a perspective, Christians would be saved by Christ while others would be saved by the Holy Spirit.

With regard to these views, the Church does not want to limit the action of the Holy Spirit to just the visible aspect of the Church. This observable dimension would include those who explicitly confess Christ's saving power. The Church does indeed have an essential visible aspect, but she is also a mystery whose reality is not fully evident to human eyes.

Still, the Church insists that the Father's sending of the Son for our salvation is inseparable from the Father's gift of the Holy Spirit. As the Congregation for the Doctrine of the Faith's Declaration *Dominus Iesus* states,

> In the New Testament, the mystery of Jesus, the Incarnate Word, constitutes the place of the Holy Spirit's presence as well as the principle of the Spirit's effusion on humanity, not only in messianic times, but also prior to his coming in history.

As in the beginning of the Church's mission, as seen in the example of Cornelius (see Acts 10), the Holy Spirit acts in invisible and mysterious ways in each person, in a way which only God sees. Nonetheless, this action of the Holy Spirit is always part of the salvation offered in Jesus Christ.

We will the discuss the nature of Christ's salvific mediation with more detail in chapter three. Suffice it for this chapter to recall the Church's clear teaching, echoing the New Testament, that Christ is the *only* Savior of the human race. As the Church stated during the Jubilee Year of 2000, in the Declaration *Dominus Iesus*, "Jesus Christ has a significance and a value for the human race and its history, which are unique and singular, proper to him alone, exclusive, universal, and absolute."

Giving this importance to Christ does not take away from the many good and noble realities found outside of Christ and outside of the Church. Rather, it is precisely through Christ's Incarnation that such human realities are elevated to their fullest meaning. Only in him do our desires for truth and goodness find their ultimate fulfillment.

CHAPTER 2

The Concept of Redemption

The word "redemption" is not often used, yet it is fundamental because it indicates the most radical liberation that God could fulfil for us, for all of humanity and for all of creation.

–Pope Francis, Audience, September 10, 2016

A. The Meaning of Redemption

In our everyday language, the words *salvation* and *redemption* can seem fairly interchangeable. But redemption is a narrower term than salvation. As we have seen in chapter one, salvation refers to the liberation which God offers to us, so as to free us from the limitations of our creaturely and fallen condition, through an invitation to share in the divine life. Redemption refers to the specific *way* by which God brings about salvation.

As in our common everyday language, in which we speak about redeeming a coupon, for example, the concept of redemption originally had an everyday use with regard to economic transactions. In the Greek world, the words redemption/redeem were used with regard to commercial exchange and indicated a liberation from slavery.

One of the Hebrew words which expresses redemption is *gaal*. The word seems to have had the original sense of "to protect." The term referred to a relative who had the responsibility of protecting or looking after the persons and property of his family. According to the Leviratic law, for example, the next of kin would be entrusted with redeeming the name of a brother who died. This next of kin would take the deceased brother's wife. The first son of this new marriage would be considered juridically to be the "son" of the deceased brother, thereby perpetuating this deceased brother's name (see Dt 25:5–6).

The fact that property and persons could be redeemed by a relative was itself a recognition of God's dominion over all creation: "The land shall not be sold in perpetuity, for the land is mine" (Lv 25:23). Due to this principle, persons and property cannot be irreversibly lost. Consequently, when a person became poor and had to sell his property, the person's closest relative had the responsibility to "redeem what his brother has sold" (Lv 25:25).

The same principle applied to persons. In the case of particularly severe debts, the person could lose his land and additionally be sold into slavery. In the Old Testament, God commands that mercy be shown toward such persons among the People of Israel. The indebted and enslaved persons might be "redeemed" or freed from their debt by one of their family members (Lv 25:48–49).

The Old Testament applies the role of redeemer to God. Just as the figure of the redeemer acted to protect his relative, God is the Redeemer who acts to protect the people to whom he has committed himself in the covenant. God shows this loving care particularly toward those who were in situations of greater vulnerability: strangers, widows, and orphans (see Ex 22:20–21).

Just as the sense of salvation has different meanings in the Old Testament, God's redeeming action also takes different forms among the People of Israel. The redemption could indicate a liberation from evil or military victory, or it could refer more specifically to the deliverance to be offered by the future messiah.

The meaning of redemption is clearer in light of the other Hebrew word which expresses this concept: *padah*. This term conveys the sense of "ransom," or acquiring the property of another by paying for it. In the Jewish law this ransom could refer to a release from a person's obligation or also the recovery of animals. In theory, anyone could pay the ransom and thereby recover what had been lost. The ancient Code of Hammurabi, a collection of Babylonian laws from nearly two millennia before Christ, also bears witness to the principle of ransom. Hence, we can see the law of ransom as responding to some basic human sensibilities: the sense of solidarity with others and the recognition of the need for forgiveness.

Applied to human persons, the concept of ransom is connected to the ancient practice of consecrating all of the firstborn children of Israel. Because the firstborn children belonged to God, these children needed to be "ransomed" by means of an animal or some form of payment. In this way, the practice of ransom acknowledged God's authority over human life.

Ransom also served as a reminder of the way God himself liberated his people from slavery in Egypt (see Ex 13:13–16). As much as this moment was a central event in the life of the Chosen People, the people looked forward to a later definitive redemption which the messiah would bring. The prophet Isaiah consoles Israel, as it suffers during its Babylonian captivity, with the promise of a future liberation which ultimately would be fulfilled in Christ: "[T]he ransomed of the LORD shall return, and come to Zion with singing; everlasting joy shall be upon their heads; they shall obtain joy and gladness, and sorrow and sighing shall flee away" (Is 51:11).

In summary, the concept of redemption, applied to the relationship between God and his people, reminds us of that debt which we have toward God. The sense of "being in debt" could refer to the material conditions of slavery which the Chosen People experienced, but also to the unpayable debt that we owe

to God for our existence. In addition, the Old Testament recognizes the particular debt which the People of Israel have as a
result of transgressions against their special covenant with God.
The covenant between God and his people, made at Mount
Sinai through the mediation of Moses, was confirmed by the
sprinkling of blood (see Ex 24:6–8). According to Jewish interpreters, this blood indicated the punishment of death which
would befall the Israelites if they failed to be faithful in their
commitment to God.

In the face of Israel's sin, Moses recognizes the need to
make *atonement* to God (see Ex 32:20). Moses asks God to
free his people from the particularly grievous debt that they
have incurred with their sin. As the American Scripture scholar
Michael Patrick Barber points out, commenting on the Old
Testament texts, "The word 'atonement' (Hebrew *kipper*) can
have the sense of 'ransom.'" This is shown in the Torah's regula-
tions for dealing with a murderer (see Nm 35:31–33), in which
"'atonement' refers to delivering a person from death by means
of a payment, that is, a 'ransom.'"

This logic of the covenant, which regards the People of
Israel, offers a helpful means for understanding the need for
redemption among all persons. The covenant of Sinai is, after all,
a development of the covenant which God made with humanity
starting with creation. In committing the first sin, Adam and
Eve break this sacred pact, and they incur the penalty of death
of which God had forewarned them (see Gn 3:3). The Book of
Genesis indicates that all of the human race, of whom Adam and
Eve are the parents, will suffer the punishment of this first act of
disobedience (3:16–19).

The description of this punishment manifests that the
presence of suffering, disordered desires, and death are a consequence of man's turning away from God's command (see Gn
3:16–19). However, precisely in this moment which reveals our

need to be ransomed from the dominion of sin, God also sets the stage for the Redemption. The account of the Fall also contains the first announcement of the Redeemer and his mother who will triumph over sin.

In the context of this prophecy of the future Savior, we can appreciate that the harsh conditions imposed upon our first parents and the whole human race are not simply an act of revenge by God. Rather, suffering and death offer us the opportunity to make an act of self-gift in love which, moved by grace, frees us from the state of sin.

In summary, while the concept of redemption emerges from the language of commercial transactions in the ancient world, this idea nonetheless expresses a deep truth about us. In our fallen state, we exist in a state of indebtedness to God. Adam and Eve freely rejected their Creator and the gift of friendship with him. As a result, we are enslaved to sin (see Jn 8:34) and are utterly helpless to escape this situation with our own powers. Nevertheless, the writings of the Old Testament continually nourish the hope of fallen man with the promise of the liberation which God would provide.

B. Errors on the Nature of Redemption

An accurate perspective on redemption requires a delicate balance in which we appreciate the dignity of human nature, the reality of sin, and the power of the grace offered by God. Without a humble adherence to God's revelation, we can easily err in understanding this mystery.

Perhaps the most familiar error regarding redemption is the position which would deny the very need of redemption from God. In light of the many noble achievements of the human person, and with a vision distorted by pride and the other effects of original sin, we can easily convince ourselves that we do not need redemption. Vatican II's *Constitution on the Church in the Modern World* describes the disorder present in our hearts due to sin, but also notes that

> no doubt many whose lives are infected with a practical materialism are blinded against any sharp insight into this kind of dramatic situation; or else, weighed down by unhappiness they are prevented from giving the matter any thought.

Within such a perspective, people can readily conclude that human effort will bring about the liberation which we long for: "Thinking they have found serenity in an interpretation of reality everywhere proposed these days," the Council continues,

> many look forward to a genuine and total emancipation of humanity wrought solely by human effort; they are convinced that the future rule of man over the earth will satisfy every desire of his heart.

Many go to the extent of saying that the concept of humanity itself is devoid of meaning, and as the Council document goes on to note, they "strive to confer a total meaning on it by their own ingenuity alone."

This temptation to bring about redemption by human effort has existed throughout history. In the first centuries after Christ, for example, the Gnostics held that the human spirit itself, since it was a kind of spark of God's own life, could redeem itself through *gnosis*—the Greek term for knowledge—of the divine mysteries. Redemption, according to this vision, involved an escape from the material world which Gnosticism views as corrupt.

Pelagianism, named for the fourth- and fifth-century British theologian Pelagius, held that our free will has the power of self-redemption without the need for grace. Pelagius denied the truth that human beings are in a fallen state in which they have an inclination to sin. According to him, original sin was the bad example given by Adam and Eve rather than a wound in human nature which is passed on to each person. In this perspective, Christ appears primarily as a good example and his work of redemption seems superfluous.

St. Augustine, the great North African bishop and Doctor of the Church, corrected Pelagius' view with his strong insistence of fallen humanity's continual need for grace. However, taken out of context, Augustine's teachings could lead to other types of errors about the Redemption. Instead of giving too much value to human effort, as in the case of Pelagius, we could also fall into the danger of giving too much attention to human sinfulness. Some, taking Augustine's teaching to an extreme, taught the doctrine of *double predestination*: God predestines the elect to eternal life and the wicked for damnation. Such a position does not leave adequate space for the reality of our free will.

Moreover, double predestination could lead to still further error regarding the meaning of Christ's redemption. The ninth-century theologian Gottshalk of Orbais, basing himself on the teaching of double predestination, said that Christ did not die for all of the human race but rather only the predestined. Although the precise details of Gottshalk's position are unclear, it is worth recalling the Council of Quiercy's rebuttal to him. The Council recalled that

> there has never been and there never will be anybody whose nature has not been assumed by Jesus Christ, Our Lord, so also there is no man, there never has been and there never will be, for whom he has not suffered.

The Council of Quierzy went on to state that this redemption will not bring about salvation if persons do not willingly receive it.

To sum up, then, the errors regarding redemption can go to two extremes, though our world manifests a great diversity of perspectives. Some deny that we are in a state of sin and need to be redeemed. Others recognize our sinful state but deny the ability of fallen man, or at least all of fallen humanity, to fully receive the gift of redemption.

C. Non-Christian Conceptions of Redemption

Apart from the question of our need for redemption, the different world religions have distinct understandings of what redemption means. As discussed in chapter one, the various systems of belief bear witness to the natural desire for salvation, though with differing conceptions of what such salvation entails.

In the Hindu religion, salvation and redemption involve a liberation from the law of *karma*, which is a law of birth followed by rebirth, involving retribution. Buddhism, on the other hand, does not have a unified sense of the meaning of reality or of the existence of God. In this perspective, redemption involves a liberation or *nirvana*. In this state, the person escapes the fragmentary and impermanent condition of existence, to achieve a radical state of emptiness. While this state cannot be precisely defined, nirvana includes a liberation from the sufferings of this world as well as freedom from all human desires. Islam does not have a concept of original sin or the Christian sense of redemption, although it does recognize our need to obtain salvation by turning to God in faith.

Although these perspectives of the great world religions are quite different among themselves and distinct from the Christian vision, we should also keep in mind that the Christian doctrine of redemption does respond to the natural religious desire found in all persons. This is seen in the various traditional and tribal religions which are not major world religions but which have their roots in ancient times. Such religions often speak of a fall of the human being from an ideal situation, and in turn foster the expectation of a redeemer-savior figure who will re-establish harmony and happiness.

D. Redemption and Salvation:
Necessity of Redemption for the Salvation of Man

In view of the various ideas about redemption described above, the nature of the Christian vision emerges more clearly. In order to reach the participation in divine life and fulfillment of the deepest human desires, which we know as salvation, we need to be liberated from the state of sin. God, in his infinite justice, is right to demand a fitting punishment for original sin and humanity's later sins. As in the cases of material poverty which required a monetary payment to fulfill the Jewish law of ransom, the whole human race needs the action of God to be lifted up from the wretchedness of sin.

God could not be compelled to carry out this action of redemption, since God is free and can't be conditioned by the human will. On the other hand, we ourselves are utterly in need of God's redeeming action. St. Thomas Aquinas, the great thirteenth-century Dominican and doctor of the church, points out that the offense of sin has a kind of infinite aspect of malice to it. This is the case, he asserts, because it is an offense against the infinite majesty of God. As a result, an act with infinite value would be required, which the human being could not perform on his own. True atonement for our sins, Aquinas concludes, would thus require an act on the part of one who is both God and man.

While keeping in mind the need to repair the offense of sin, we should always try to see redemption within the deeper context of God's *covenant* with his people. From the beginning of creation, God has committed himself to raising the human person to participation in the divine life. From this point of view, that of God's own loving plan for the human race, we *can* say that there is a necessity for God to redeem us. Redemption is a necessary form which God's love for humanity takes.

We can also affirm that the concept of redemption, in comparison with other terms which express God's action—such as salvation, justification, or reconciliation—expresses God's love in a particularly powerful way. Redemption shows, as the American theologian David Moessner points out, "the necessity for God to be both 'victim' and 'hero,' to create new life precisely through God's own death." God brings to fulfillment the goodness present in the human acts of redemption or ransom. Just as we are moved when someone generously sacrifices himself or herself for us, the redemption carried out by Christ offers a moving and tangible manifestation of God's desire to offer us salvation.

God chooses to be faithful to his covenant with humanity despite our unfaithfulness. He chose to draw close to us not simply from the outside or by means of intermediaries, but by becoming one of us. In the following chapters, we will seek to examine this mystery of God's love, which fulfills the demands of justice. In this process, as St. John Paul II noted,

> the God of creation is revealed as the God of redemption, as the God who is 'faithful to himself' (see 1 Thess 5:24), and faithful to his love for man and the world, which he revealed on the day of creation. His is a love that does not draw back before anything that justice requires in him.

This love can fully heal the wounds present in our souls because of sin, but more fundamentally, God's charity responds to our essential calling to love. Study and meditation on the truth of redemption should therefore lead to a wonder at the mystery of God, but also to a deeper appreciation of the greatness of our dignity.

CHAPTER 3

The Mediation of Christ

The Church's Magisterium, faithful to divine revelation, reasserts that Jesus Christ is the mediator and the universal redeemer: "The Word of God, through whom all things were made, was made flesh, so that as perfect man he could save all men and sum up all things in himself."

—Congregation for the Doctrine of the Faith,
Declaration Dominus Iesus

A. The Concept of Mediation

The notion of *mediation* is essential for understanding how God brings about the salvation and redemption of humanity. A precise understanding of this term is also necessary for a correct appreciation of the Church and her activity.

The concept of mediation is familiar to us in our culture. A mediator is someone who stands in between two parties that are in conflict with one another. The two parties might be in a serious dispute, to the point that they are not easily able to communicate with each other. Still, they might be willing to talk with a mediator, and through such dialogue they might achieve reconciliation.

This more everyday sense of mediation is the most original one. The Hebrew Scriptures, and later the New Testament, took up the notion of mediation as it was already present in the ancient Greek world. In this Hellenic context, the mediator was a neutral party between two other parties and one whom both sides could trust. This role is connected with another sense of the term: the mediator is one who can guarantee agreements.

Just as in our contemporary culture, in which mediation can serve as an alternative to official legal proceedings, in ancient times the mediator acted outside of the legal process.

At first glance, this word might not seem to be the most adequate for describing the relationship between God and his people. God is present everywhere. St. Augustine later acknowledged that, even in his moments of wandering from God, God was constantly present: "You were more inward to me than my most inward part." Many people today have difficulty with the idea of mediation, precisely because they think that it means that something is "getting in the way" of this immediate relationship with God.

As much as we might naturally resist the idea of mediation in our relationship with God, the very identity of God and of the human person makes some form of mediation indispensable. As God says to Moses, "[Y]ou cannot see my face; for man shall not see me and live" (Ex 33:20). As Christians, we hope to have in heaven the immediate perception of God's glory, known as the beatific vision. Still, in the present human condition our awareness of God is necessarily mediated in one way or another. God always remains, as the twentieth-century German theologian Michael Schmaus observed, "an ineffable mystery":

> Even when he does show himself to us, his mystery does not become thereby transparent—not that he wants to keep anything from us, but his very nature renders it impossible. He can grant us a glimpse into the veiled mystery which he is, but it still remains a mystery.

Even in the case of Christ, God's definitive revelation to mankind, the glory of God's divinity remains hidden alongside Christ's humanity. Thus, God speaks to us in ways which necessarily fall short of the full mystery of who God is.

Along with this natural distance between God and his creatures, sin also has created a real separation between us and our Creator. The account of man's first sin expresses this distance through the image of the first man and woman hiding from God, as well as the expulsion from the Garden of Eden (see Gn 3:8, 3:24). Through our free choice to reject God, God and humanity become like two parties in conflict with one another.

The account of the first sin, as we know, is just an initial moment in the history of God's relationship with us. God desires to rebuild this relationship, and he does so through the mediation of different signs. These signs express God's presence and his will, but also the response of the People to God's word. For the Chosen People, this mediation occurred in a very special way through the *Law* and *worship* established by God.

Alongside this mediation, the Old Testament frequently describes certain persons who are called to adhere to his plan and also to become instruments for developing God's covenant with his people. *Moses* is the prime example. By means of him, God renews the alliance he had made with Abraham and establishes the Law. Moses passes on God's message to the Chosen People, but he himself also brings to God the needs of the people. They recognize that he is the one fitted to hear God's word and speak to Yahweh on their behalf: "You speak to us, and we will hear; but let not God speak to us, lest we die" (Ex 20:19).

The second great figure of mediation in the Old Testament is the *Servant of Yahweh*. This Servant is described in four fragments within the second part of the Book of Isaiah. He is a mysterious figure who does not possess a majestic or glorious outward appearance; to the contrary he is harshly treated and "they made his grave with the wicked" (Is 53:9). Despite these appearances, the Servant is God's chosen one, who will bring his salvation to the Chosen People as well as all nations (see Is 49:6). The Servant's sufferings are a source of healing and forgiveness for sin (see Is 53:5).

The figures of Moses and the Servant of Yahweh show us the profound power of mediation found in the Hebrew Scriptures, but also the deep humility which should characterize those who act as mediators. The Book of Numbers testifies that "the man Moses was very meek, more than all men that were on the face of the earth" (Nm 12:3). Similarly, the Servant of Yahweh speaks with mildness (see Is 42:2). Moreover, this Servant "had no form or comeliness that we should look at him, and no beauty that we should desire him. He was despised and rejected by men; a man of sorrows, and acquainted with grief" (Is 53:2–3). In both cases, the humility of the mediator stands in stark contrast with the radiant glory of God which is revealed by him. There is no danger of confusing the mediator with God himself.

In light of this logic, we can understand why Old Testament Hebrew does not have a word which is equivalent to "mediation." The absence of this term is part of the distinctiveness of the Old Testament's perspective on God and the world. The ancient world was filled with belief in mediators who were demigods and who served as intercessors. These pagan mediators were associated with God's action in the world. For example, they were thought to keep heaven above the earth. In this context, there was the risk of associating mediation with a pantheistic vision, which blurs the relationship between God and his creation.

In contrast to these pagan ideas, the God of Israel is one and absolutely transcendent. Aware of our tendency to put lesser beings in the place of the one God, the Old Testament understandably refrains from speaking about mediation, at least in an explicit way. The Creation accounts manifest God to be all-powerful. Yahweh creates by his own power and not with the help of intermediate beings as in other religions.

The Law of Israel did acknowledge the human reality of mediation, in which arbitrators acted as intermediaries between two parties of equal standing (see Ex 21:22; Jb 9:33). In the case of God and his people, it is clear that we are not dealing with two entities that are equivalent. The Book of Job manifests an awareness of the Greek sense of mediation when Job expresses his desire for an "umpire" (Jb 9:33) between God and himself. However, he comes to realize that God himself is this vindicator who will bring him life (Jb 19:25). God himself therefore appears as the "mediator" between himself and humanity, and this action foreshadows the perfect mediation offered by Christ.

To summarize, Old Testament revelation expresses the fundamental truth about mediation, but does not prefer to use the actual language of mediation. Nevertheless, revelation reveals how God wills and chooses creatures to cooperate in the actualization of his plans: angels, messengers, prophets, kings, and priests. These persons, who act as mediators without being called such, are shown clearly not to be divine and not to be confused with God. They are instruments called to be totally at the service of Yahweh.

In ancient times, both within and outside of the Bible, the task of human mediators was divided into three distinct roles, as indicated by the Latin term *munus triplex*: the king, the priest, and the prophet. The king was seen as a god or a son of god, who received authority from God and acted in the name of the people toward god. In this sense, the role of the king could intersect with the role of the priest, who had the role of prayer and sacrifice for the people. Distinct was the function of the prophet, who was a man of God and miracle-worker.

B. Existence and Nature of the Mediation of Christ

As we have seen, in general the Old Testament resists speaking about mediation with regard to God. The same is true in much of the New Testament. The word *mediation* is not used in the Gospels. Still, the teachings of the Gospels indicate that Jesus carries out the role of a mediator. Moreover, Christ brings this function to its fulfillment. He is the one who is truly able to act as intermediary between God and man, and bring about reconciliation. He undoes the distance which we have created between ourselves and our Creator by sin.

The Gospels express this reality in varied ways. St. Matthew presents Christ as the New Moses. As in the case of Moses, the great mediator of the Old Testament, Christ's teaching is associated with a *mountain*. In ancient times, the mountain was considered to be the place where heaven and earth met. In the Old Testament, the mountain is the special place where God reveals himself to Moses and later Elijah (see Ex 3:15; 1 Kgs 19:8–13). On Mount Sinai, in the midst of fire, thunder, and a cloud of darkness, Moses receives the law to pass on to the Chosen People (Ex chapters 19—20 and 34).

In the Gospels, too, the mountain is the special place where Jesus enters into intimate dialogue with his Father (Lk 6:12). He speaks with the Father in the perfect communion of his divine nature, which involves a closeness which even Moses was not able to attain (see Ex 33:20). From this intimacy with the Father, Christ proclaims the Beatitudes upon a mountain, and in so doing he reveals the new Torah, the definitive Law intended for all humanity. Christ echoes the demands of the Law given by Moses but makes these demands even greater, and claims to speak with stronger authority (see Mt 5).

Christ shows the power of his mediation not simply in his presence on the mountain, but also by coming down from the mountain to the *plain* (Lk 6:17). In the Old Testament, the Chosen People remained at the foot of the mountain and from there they received the special revelation given to Moses (Ex 19:17). St. Luke emphasizes Christ's descent to the plain and in doing so he shows the way Christ has come to bring the revelation of God to all persons.

The proclamation of Christ as the *Son of God* expresses, in a particularly powerful way, the way Christ perfectly realizes the role of mediator. This sonship is not a vague term but expresses an intimate unity and equality with God. Christ is the only-begotten Son, and only through him do we have access to the divine life. As St. Matthew states in an important passage which reveals Christ's identity, "All things have been delivered to me by my Father; and no one knows the Son except the Father, and no one knows the Father except the Son and any one to whom the Son chooses to reveal him" (Mt 11:27). With these words, the Evangelist describes a unique relationship of knowledge and love between the Father and the Son, which implies a genuine sharing of life.

St. John describes the unique mediation of Christ even more fully in his Gospel. While "[n]o one has ever seen God" (Jn 1:18), Christ, who is the definitive *Word* of God (Jn 1:1), has revealed the divine mysteries. As language serves a mediating function in a conversation between two persons, the person of Christ is the essential mediation by which God speaks to us. This mediation does not simply occur by the transmission of knowledge, not even by moral and religious truth, but by the communication of divine life: "For the law was given through Moses; grace and truth came through Jesus Christ" (Jn 1:17).

In his account of the Last Supper, the beloved disciple expresses this mediation in a particularly clear-cut way. In contrast with the other religious leaders who claim to act in the name of God (see Jn 10:8; 5:43), the Evangelist records the clear affirmation of Christ: "I am the way, and the truth, and the life; no one comes to the Father, but by me" (Jn 14:6). The central guiding thread of the fourth Gospel is that of bringing the reader to faith in Christ, so as pass over from a state of sin to a new condition of friendship with God (see Jn 8:34; 20:31). In the Book of Revelation, St. John describes Christ as the only who can open "the scroll and its seven seals" (5:5). With this language from the last book of the Bible, the

Evangelist shows that Christ reveals to us not just the mystery of God but also the hidden workings of God's plan in history.

In describing the mediation carried out by Christ, the New Testament paints a portrait of mediation which goes beyond the limitations of the Greek conception. The Hellenic view implied that the mediator was a neutral party who was therefore able to bring together parties in conflict. In the ancient pagan view of the universe, mediators were equally the source of ruin and salvation. Christ's mediation, on the other hand, does not involve any kind of neutrality or indifference. His mediation is the fruit of God's infinite love for us and undoes the ruin brought about by Adam's sin.

In his suffering and death, Christ manifests in a supreme manner the love which motivates his mediation. When the Evangelists describe these moments, they show that Christ fulfills the type of mediation foreshadowed by the Suffering Servant in Isaiah. This figure offers his life so as to bring about our friendship with God (see Mk 10:45; Jn 1:29). Among other texts, St. John records the prophecy of the high priest, unknowingly fulfilled through the action of the religious leaders, that "Jesus should die for the nation, and not for the nation only, but to gather into one the children of God who are scattered abroad" (11:51–52). Jesus himself freely and willingly accepts this sacrifice of himself, fully aware of its salvific purpose. As he affirms: "I, when I am lifted up from the earth, will draw all men to myself" (Jn 12:32).

St. Paul's preaching contributed greatly to showing the centrality of Christ's passion, death, and resurrection in the process of mediation. With this emphasis, the Apostle to the Gentiles does not intend to take away importance from the entirety of the life of Christ. Still, he—along with the early Church—was keenly aware that a new era of salvation had come about, precisely through Christ's offering up of himself on the Cross and his resurrection from the dead.

In summary, then, Christ's role as a mediator of salvation is fundamental to the gospel message. Christ fulfills the role of mediator found in the pagan world and at the same time transforms it. In the Greek world, the demigods involved in mediation were primarily focused on carrying out the cosmic functioning of the universe. Christ, by contrast, reconciles us with God, and through this work of salvation the entire universe is renewed. By his entire life, and particularly through his passion and death, he brings the saving mystery of God to man.

C. Mediation and Hypostatic Union

Mediation is a key concept in the New Testament, even if this particular term is not often used. The Letter to the Galatians seems to use the word *mediator* in a negative sense. St. Paul appears to show that the law is imperfect precisely because it came through a mediator, that is, through the angels (Gal 3:19). Within such a vision, an action that is mediated would be less directly carried out by God.

However, the profound reality of Christ's incarnation allows St. Paul to give mediation a new and different meaning. As the apostle states in the First Letter to Timothy: "For there is one God, and there is one mediator between God and men, the man Christ Jesus, who gave himself as a ransom for all, the testimony to which was borne at the proper time" (1 Tm 2:5–6).

In this passage, the word *man* indicates the central role of the Incarnation in mediation. Through the Incarnation, mediation no longer implies that an intermediary stands between us and God. This is because Christ is both fully man and fully God. Through this mediation, all of humanity can partake of God's salvation. The context of St. Paul's affirmation that Christ is mediator is God's will for "all men to be saved and to come to the knowledge of the truth" (1 Tm 2:4).

Christ fulfills the role of mediation through the *hypostatic union*. This union refers to the union of the divine and human natures in the one person of Christ. The term expresses the truth that Christ has both divine and human natures within his one personhood. This union occurs without a "mixing" of the divine and human. The human and divine natures remain distinct from one another.

The Fathers of the Church strenuously defended these truths about Christ against many misunderstandings. They did so with the awareness that the union of the human and divine natures in Christ, along with the distinction of these natures, was the path through which Christ could act as mediator for our salvation. Christ truly has taken on a human nature, without leaving his divine nature, so that we might be raised to God.

As Pope St. Leo remarked in his important letter explaining the identity of Christ, Christ's birth,

> which took place in time took nothing from, and added nothing to that divine and eternal birth, but expended itself wholly on the restoration of man who had been deceived: in order that he might both vanquish death and overthrow by his strength, the Devil who possessed the power of death. For we should not now be able to overcome the author of sin and death unless He took our nature on Him and made it His own.

The reality of Christ's incarnation has brought about a new possibility of mediation for the human race. With this event, one who is fully man can also act as fully God and thus fully make atonement for man's sin. Through the hypostatic union, Christ becomes the head of mankind and therefore the natural representative of the human race. This representative function is connected to the solidarity which exists among all the members of the human race. St. Paul describes this solidarity in the letter to the Romans

(5:12–21). Adam's sin has led all of mankind into a state of sin; Christ in contrast is the source of redemption for all humanity.

By virtue of his unique identity, Christ has the particular role of *interceding*, or making petition, to God on behalf of the human race. He intercedes as a member of the human race and at the same time one who has divine power. This petition to God fulfills, at the level of the whole human race, the intercession which Moses made on behalf of the Chosen People (Ex 32:30–22).

Intercession is not simply one more action which Christ carries out. Christ's petition to the Father on our behalf is a characteristic of his mission on earth (see Jn 11:41–42; chapter 17). This action expresses how Jesus' entire life and person are directed to the Father for our good and our salvation. The Letter to the Hebrews reveals that the risen and glorified Christ perpetually intercedes in heaven: "[H]e is able for all time to save those who draw near to God through him, since he always lives to make intercession for them" (7:25).

This same letter, later on, gives further expression to the new mediation brought about through Christ's humanity. The sacred author recognizes that the Incarnation does away with the separation between God and humanity caused by sin. Through "the new and living way which he opened for us through the curtain, that is, through his flesh" (Heb 10:20), Christians have access to God which had not been possible in the Old Law and its prescriptions.

The "curtain" mentioned in this passage refers to the veil of the tabernacle and later of the temple. This cloth had the function of separating the inner holy part, the "Holy of Holies," from the rest of the sanctuary. There seems to be a connection here between the "curtain" which is Christ's flesh and the temple veil which is torn in two at the moment of Christ's death (Mk 15:38). In contrast to the temple veil which blocks access to God, the veil which is Christ's flesh allows believers to enter with new intimacy into the divine life.

In this manner, Christ mediates a covenant which is "better" than the Law passed on by Moses, "since it is enacted on better promises" (Heb 8:6). While the former covenant could not truly bridge the gap between humanity and God, the covenant brought about by Christ has power to "purify" the "conscience from dead works to serve the living God" (Heb 9:14).

In this new covenant, Christ has the role of guarantor (see Heb 7:22), which was part of the role of a mediator in the Greek world. Christ's role as mediator in this context conveys the sense, as the twentieth-century German theologian Albrecht Oepke pointed out, of "a contracted obligation whose fulfillment Jesus guarantees, in a sense by sharing the debt." This connotation allows us to appreciate the relation between Christ's role as mediator and the redemption which pays the debt of our sin. Christ has offered to us a guarantee of redemption, and has done so through his own death as mediator.

D. Mediator and Mediators

Given the completely unique way in which Christ acts as mediator, we might ask what role human beings can have as mediators in the Church's salvific mission. Many people today who recognize the singular role of Christ have a hard time applying the term *mediator* to human beings. This issue has been a key area of difference of perspective with a number of Protestant communities, who do not accept that the Church and her members might have a mediating role.

Given the earlier overview of Scripture on this topic, we can understand such a difficulty. Scripture is very careful in using the term mediator. We should also be careful in ascribing the term to persons other than Christ. Nonetheless, God's revelation before and in Christ shows that human mediation is an essential part of God's plan for the salvation of all.

The Second Vatican Council's Dogmatic Constitution on the Church, *Lumen Gentium*, sought to more clearly express this truth in a way which might be more understandable to separated Christians. In the document, the Council recognizes that Christ is the "one Mediator" who "established and continually sustains here on earth His holy Church." It is through this Church, the text continues, that Christ "communicated truth and grace to all."

However, the existence and power of the one mediator, Christ, does not exclude the possibility of secondary mediators. In fact, the Old Testament image of the Servant of Yahweh can be understood not simply as referring to the messiah, but to all of the People of God. All of these people are called to be "a light to the nations," so that God's "salvation may reach to the end of the earth" (Is 49:6). This prophecy is fulfilled in the mediation of Christ but also in the mediation of the Church, the new People of God and Christ's Mystical Body.

The human mediation exercised by the Church, according to the will of Christ, is a continuation of the supernatural dynamic brought about by Christ's Incarnation. By this mystery of the Word-made-flesh, as the Second Vatican Council's Constitution *Dei Verbum* affirms in words inspired by Scripture, "the invisible God out of the abundance of His love speaks to men as friends and lives among them, so that He may invite and take them into fellowship with Himself." In raising men and women to the divine life, God desires to make them instruments for passing on this same divine life to others. He wants persons to freely participate in spreading the redemption of Christ, and thus reconcile fallen humanity with God. Through the mystery of the Church, the following words of Christ can be applied to all of Christ's disciples: "He who hears you hears me" (Lk 10:16).

Thus, the very mystery of the mediation of Christ himself also implies that other human beings can share in the reality of mediation. This applies in the first place to the Blessed Virgin Mary, whom Christ has willed to be the mediatrix of all graces. The Constitution *Lumen Gentium* states that the mediation of Mary

> in no wise obscures or diminishes this unique mediation of Christ, but rather shows His power. For all the salvific influence of the Blessed Virgin on men originates, not from some inner necessity, but from the divine pleasure. It flows forth from the superabundance of the merits of Christ, rests on His mediation, depends entirely on it and draws all its power from it.

Christ shows forth his power in leading us to partake of the divine life and to pass on this life. In a particular way which is proper to them, ordained ministers share in the role of Christ, the one mediator, when they announce the gospel and administer the sacraments while acting in the very person of Christ himself. At the same time, the full mystery of the Church means that every Christian is, as St. Josemaría Escrivá comments, "an apostle—that is what a Christian is, when he knows that he has been grafted onto Christ, made one with Christ, in baptism." Each Christian is called to share in Christ's priesthood, through baptism and confirmation, and thereby partake in Christ's mediation. As Escrivá continues, "Each of us is to be *ipse Christus*: Christ himself. He is the one mediator between God and man. And we make ourselves one with him in order to offer all things, with him, to the Father." Christ's unique and exclusive mediation shows its power precisely in that he allows us to receive his saving action and serve as mediators for others.

CHAPTER 4

The Three Offices of Christ

These are the three chief views which are vouchsafed to us of His Mediatorial office; and it is often observed that none before Him has, even in type or resemblance, borne all three characters. Melchizedek, for instance, was a priest and a king, but not a prophet. David was prophet and king, but not a priest. Jeremiah was priest and prophet, but not a king. Christ was Prophet, Priest, and King.

—St. John Henry Newman

As we have seen, Christ is the definitive mediator willed by God for granting salvation to the human race. While this is a fundamental truth of Christ's identity, Sacred Scripture usually prefers to express the reality of mediation in various ways, which don't involve the terminology of mediation. In this chapter, we will examine three fundamental religious categories used in the Old Testament to describe the mysterious reality of mediation: king, prophet, and priest. Jesus unites and fulfills each of these roles in his person.

These three offices of mediation took on an important role in the covenant which God established with his people through Moses. Along with the special revelation of God's ordinances to Moses, there arose the need for human institutions to pass on the covenant. From the perspective of the covenant, we can appreciate the *mediating* aspect of these three roles. The king, the prophet, and the priest are not significant for who they are but for what they convey. These roles exist to pass on the gifts of God to his people.

A. The Royal or Pastoral Ministry of Christ

From ancient times, and not just in the Bible, the concept of kingship had a connection with God. Kings were viewed as God's representatives. In this context, the revelation of the true God would purify the idea of kingship. In the Old Testament, the king is not equated with God but is an instrument who must be at the service of God's will.

In fact, the human figure of a king does not form part of the original covenant of God with his Chosen People. The People of Israel were familiar with kingship from neighboring peoples. But at first, it was God himself who fulfilled this role and not any human being. Royalty was associated with God and his transcendence, rather than with a human king. With the covenant given through Moses at Mount Sinai, God established his people as "a kingdom of priests and a holy nation" (Ex 19:6). The ark of the covenant was God's royal throne.

A king is granted to Israel only with the displeasure of the prophet Samuel and the reluctance of God himself (1 Sm 8:6–9). With this disapproval, revelation shows the ambiguity of human kingship. Samuel warns the people of the perils which will come from having a human king. Among other demands a king will make upon the people,

> [H]e will take your sons and appoint them to his chariots and to be his horsemen, and to run before his chariots; and he will appoint for himself commanders of thousands and commanders of fifties, and some to plow his ground and to reap his harvest, and to make his implements of war and the equipment of his chariots. (1 Sm 8:11–12)

The later history of Israel would bear witness to the evils that would come upon the people because of kings who turned away from God's covenant.

However, despite God's initial negative reaction to the reality of kingship, we should not see this institution as essentially corrupt. God in fact does grant the people's request for a king, and later makes kingship part of his promises. Certainly, in Israel and elsewhere, there was the danger of substituting trust in God with trust in royalty. At the same, the people's insistent request for a king manifests a natural human desire for authority.

The need for authority in society has been a constant throughout history and is also very much present today. For example, many people around us are frustrated to see politicians not being able to come to an agreement with one another. In the case of ancient Israel, the People of God recognized that having a king would give their nation the organizational unity which they desired for protection against the neighboring peoples.

We should also note that the People of Israel recognize that a king must be granted to them by God, by means of the prophet Samuel. Their petition shows their awareness that kingship in Israel was a human institution which required God's consent. Such was the case, even if in practice kings would depart from God's plan. The practice of anointing kings with oil was a way of expressing the dependence of kingly power upon God.

During the time of King David, the role of the monarchy achieved a level of political organization in Israel which was similar to neighboring countries. As in the case of other peoples, the king had the role of defending the people of Israel from their enemies and promoting the well-being of the nation.

At the same time, the king of Israel was radically different from the surrounding kings. He was not a "god" but at the service of the true God and of God's covenant with his people. The king of Israel was specially favored by God, but if he was not faithful, he would lose this favor. The kings after David would indeed fail in their loyalty to God and suffer the consequences. The prophet Hosea announces the end of kingship (Hos 3:4), and this would come to pass with the destruction of the temple in 587 BC.

The kingship of Israel, despite its apparent failure, paved the way for the full and eternal kingship of Jesus Christ. The prophets had foretold a new king who would come from the lineage of David (2 Sm 7:16 and Jer 23:5). This future king would bring about victory and a new age of prosperity and peace for Israel (see Is 9:1–6; 11:1–9).

While foretelling this king, the prophets would also purify the peoples' understanding of the kingdom of God and kingship. Kingship became less associated with earthly rule and more connected to faithfulness to God's law. As seen in the Book of Daniel, the meaning of kingship became more eternal, universal, and focused on the future age. However, at the same time, the expectation of a messiah retained a strong political aspect. The Jews at the time of Jesus longed for a messiah who would liberate them from subjugation to the Roman Empire.

Given this outlook, it is not surprising that Christ did not present himself explicitly as a king. Living in the midst of the Roman Empire, the early Christians were understandably hesitant to use a kingly title for Christ. Nevertheless, Christ's identity as king is an essential part of the gospel message. The archangel Gabriel proclaims that Christ, from the moment of his conception, will take the throne of David and establish a kingdom that will have no end (Lk 1:32–33).

The Gospels show us clearly that Christ's kingship does not line up with the earthly sense of kingship. In fact, Christ flees when he realizes that the crowds "were about to come and take him by force to make him king" (Jn 6:15). The kingdom is only revealed to the humble and childlike (see Mt 11:25; 18:3).

When Jesus does announce himself to be the king foretold by the prophets, he is accused of blasphemy (Mt 26:63–66).

Many people today, as in the time of Jesus, have a hard time accepting Christ's kingship. They easily confuse it with what they believe to be a desire for political dominion on the part of Christ or his Church. However, the revealed truth is that Christ's kingdom "is not from the world" (Jn 18:36). It is a spiritual kingdom and is not opposed to earthly kingdoms, except when these worldly kingdoms rise up against God and instead adhere to the kingship of Satan, "the ruler of this world" (Jn 12:31).

If the kingship of Christ is not a political one, what does it mean to say that Christ is king? Fundamentally, the concept of Christ's kingship is another way of articulating the *salvation* which God offers to his Chosen People and to all humanity. In relation to Christ, we should understand the notions of dominion and authority, so closely connected to kingship, in a spiritual sense.

This spiritual meaning is not just a literary figure; it expresses the fullest meaning of dominion in a way which goes far beyond an earthly vision. Through Christ, God offers us the possibility of freedom from sin and the opportunity for the reign of God to exist in our souls and in society. As Pius XI affirmed, Christ "is the salvation of the individual, in him is the salvation of society. . . . He is the author of happiness and true prosperity for every man and for every nation."

The fullness of this kingship will only be revealed at the end of time, and remains veiled in history. Even so, Christ fulfills the role of king from the first moment of his existence. His kingship is founded on the hypostatic union. Through this union by which God takes on a human nature, Christ has power over all creatures, and all owe him their adoration. In his public ministry, Christ claims the authority to establish laws and serve as judge. In the Sermon on the Mount, his capacity to give laws supersedes the authority of Moses (Mt 5—7). Christ affirms that the Father "has given all judgment to the Son" (Jn 5:22). Through his miracles, Jesus demonstrates that "the kingdom of God has come upon you" (Lk 11:20).

Christ's kingship does not simply mean that he is the instrument for bringing about the kingdom, or that he rules the kingdom. Christ himself *is* the kingdom. In his humanity there is the full dominion of God's will, which is the true significance of God's kingdom. Through the language of kingship, the Bible gives a profound expression to the rich significance of salvation. As St. Josemaría Escrivá comments:

> Truth and justice, peace and joy in the Holy Spirit. That is the kingdom of Christ: the divine activity which saves men and which will reach its culmination when history ends and the Lord comes from the heights of paradise finally to judge men.

B. The Prophetic Ministry of Christ

Today, it is common for people to turn to other persons who can offer them advice regarding God's will, for example religious ministers or other experienced persons. Non-Christians and non-believers have a whole set of other persons to whom they might turn, whether they be religious leaders, pundits on social media, or even psychics. We human beings recognize our own inadequacy to judge weighty matters, and we seek the advice of others.

The same impulse was also present in ancient times. It was common to look to persons such as *oracles*, who practiced divination and who might facilitate communication with higher beings. One would consult such persons before an important undertaking.

This was the original sense of "prophet." The Greek word expresses the function of "declaring, proclaiming, making known."

The word itself implies the function of *mediation*. The prophet does not speak on his own, but rather is one who proclaims a message which he receives from the divine realm.

This connotation of prophet is also central for Sacred Scripture. The Old Testament uses different Hebrew words as equivalents to prophet and employs these terms in varied senses. The key element is the *Word* of Yahweh which the prophet must transmit. This "Word" is not simply information but is closely associated with the presence and power of God. The prophet is not just someone who passes on wisdom. He is someone who passes on a living and vital force which, in a certain way, takes possession of him.

The vocation of the prophet Jeremiah is one of many examples which reveal the great mystery of the prophet's mission. Jeremiah realizes his own unworthiness to carry out the prophetic office, but God reminds him that the initiative belongs to God himself: "[T]o all to whom I send you you shall go, and whatever I command you you shall speak" (Jer 1:7). The symbolic gesture of God touching the prophet expresses the special action of God which is always beyond the prophet's own capabilities: "Then the LORD put forth his hand and touched my mouth; and the LORD said to me, 'Behold, I have put my words in your mouth.'" (Jer 1:9). Similar gestures are found in the vocation of other prophets (see Is 6:7; Ez 2:8–3:3; Dn 10:16).

These words of God have a message for his people, but also bring about God's action of salvation or destruction. After placing his speech in Jeremiah's mouth, God appoints the prophet "over nations and over kingdoms, to pluck up and to break down, to destroy and to overthrow, to build and to plant" (Jer 1:10).

Here, we can see how the prophet acts as a special instrument by which God carries out a dialogue with his people. This role distinguishes the prophet from the other figures of mediation.

The king has the particular task of protecting the people from enemies and the priest has the role of interpreting the Law and overseeing worship. The prophet, by contrast, conveys the living word of God, which expresses God's will for his people at a particular moment in time.

The original sense of prophet, as one who speaks the message of God, is related to one of the more common understandings we have of this term. We often think of the prophet as someone who is able to tell the future. This specific sense of prophet and prophecy has come about with Christianity. This signification is present in the Old Testament, within which the ability to tell the future is an important sign which distinguishes true from false prophets: "[W]hen a prophet speaks in the name of the LORD, if the word does not come to pass or come true, that is a word which the LORD has not spoken" (Dt 18:22).

In the Old Testament, among other qualities, the capacity to point toward the future is a distinguishing characteristic of the prophet. The priest looks to the Law which has been received, and the king looks to the immediate government of his people. Prophets, in distinction from these roles, have a message for the present moment as well as a unique gift for looking beyond the present. They remind the People of God of the future judgment that God will realize, but they also tell of the salvation and renewal that God will carry out. Their message has relevance for the present circumstances, but at the same time looks toward a much fuller and richer future which God will bring about.

The New Testament manifests that Jesus Christ is not only the chosen King and Messiah promised by God, but also a prophet. He is the prophet of the stature of Moses who was promised by God, who would proclaim a divine message to which the people had to listen (see Dt 18:15–19; Jn 5:46). Our Lord's role as a prophet was more evident to his contemporaries than was his kingship. Seeing his miracles, the crowds exclaim that "A great prophet has arisen among us!" and "God has visited his people!" (Lk 7:16)

Because Christ's role as prophet is so evident, it is crucial to understand the precise way in which he is a prophet. When the apostles remark that some say Jesus is a prophet, Jesus indicates that this title does not express his full identity. He is more than a prophet. He is, as Peter confesses moved by God's grace, "the Christ, the Son of the living God" (Mt 16:16).

In light of this truth, we can understand why the early Church did not put a lot of emphasis on Jesus' role as a prophet. Since there were many prophets in the Jewish and pagan world, the word did not really express the uniqueness of Christ. Titles such as "Son of God" or "Christ" were better for articulating who Jesus really is.

Still, Christ's unique way of being a prophet gives us important insight into his saving and mediating work. Christ brings the prophetic mission to a new and higher level. While each prophet is sent to announce a specific communication from God in a particular circumstance, Christ is the definitive message of God to the entire human race. In him, as the Second Vatican Council's *Constitution on Divine Revelation* stated, "the full revelation of the supreme God is brought to completion."

The prophet's awareness of being sent with a message from God applies in a particular way to Christ's prophetic mission. Like the prophets, Jesus can say that "the word which you hear is not mine but the Father's who sent me" (Jn 14:24). This is because Christ's humanity is completely at the service of the divine will. Not just in his words but in all of his actions, Christ perfectly reveals God and conveys God's will for mankind. Like the prophets of the Old Testament, Christ's prophetic message is not simply intellectual but has dynamic force. Going far beyond these prophets, Jesus offers to us a sharing in God's own life. He proclaims a truth which has the capacity to set us free, in the full freedom of love (see Jn 8:32 and Gal 5:13).

C. The Priestly Mediation of Jesus Christ

The Evangelists do not directly identify Jesus Christ as a priest. Giving Christ this identity might easily have led to confusion between the mission of Jesus Christ and the priesthood of the Old Covenant. But with the necessary clarifications, priesthood is another important category for understanding Christ's salvific mediation.

Just as in the case of prophets and kings, priests were present in ancient times among both pagans and the Israelites. Originally, the priest had a role which was similar to that of the prophet. He was a person who served as mediator through whom others could enter into contact with God. At first, this task was not the role of a specific group of people but could be carried out by the head of the family.

In time, the specific office of the priest emerged. The priest was under the authority of the king but specifically dedicated to the worship of God. As part of the covenant, Moses consecrated Aaron and his sons as priests (Ex 29). The entire tribe of Levi shared to some degree in this identity. The special mission of the priests was to help the Chosen People respond to their covenant with God, through observance of the Law and worship. They blessed the people, carried out sacrifices, and watched over matters related to liturgy.

The priesthood shows us another way in which human beings seek *mediation* in their relationship with God. While the prophet helped the people attain knowledge of God, the priests performed the mediation necessary so that the people could respond to God's message. Their existence shows that the People of God were in need of an intermediary so as to fulfill the command to "love the LORD your God with all your heart, and with all your soul, and with all your might" (Dt 6:5).

However, history would show that the Old Testament priesthood was never fully able to bring the people in contact with God. The author of the Letter to the Hebrews recognizes that the sacrifices of the Old Law can never completely make up for sin (Heb 9:9, 10:2–4). The First Book of Samuel contains a harsh condemnation of the sons of Eli, priests of the sanctuary at Shiloh, who have sought their own self-interest rather than the service of God (1 Sm 2:27–34). We can see this reprimand as a more general critique of the various abuses committed by priests.

In the midst of this sad situation, God announces a new beginning: "I will raise up for myself a faithful priest, who shall do according to what is in my heart and in my mind" (1 Sm 2:35). St. Augustine comments that these words manifest the rejection of the Levitical priesthood and the promise of a new priesthood. The prophecy, Augustine notes, shows that the priesthood of Aaron was only a shadow and figure of the eternal priesthood of Christ.

The priesthood before Christ, then, manifested mankind's desire for a mediator to help us adore God. In the case of the Old Testament, the priesthood also shows God's desire to lead us toward himself by means of human instruments. But only Christ's priestly mission and perfect sacrifice on the Cross would fulfill the true meaning of the priesthood. Through Christ and his gift of the Holy Spirit, human beings would be able to perform true worship "in spirit and truth" (Jn 4:23).

The priesthood of Christ is not in the line of the Old Testament priesthood. This latter priesthood was passed on through a specific family lineage. Christ was born of the tribe of Judah, so he did not have a share in the priesthood of Aaron or his descendants. The Letter to the Hebrews describes Christ as a priest not of Aaron, but in the line of Melchizedek. Melchizedek, the king of Jerusalem, blessed Abraham, and in return Abraham offered him tithes (Gn 14:18–20). In these actions, the author of Hebrews sees a superior priesthood to that of the Chosen People (Heb 7:1–7).

Melchizedek's priesthood is an eternal priesthood, as foretold in Psalm 110: "You are a priest for ever after the order of Melchizedek" (verse 4). Since the Book of Genesis does not provide information about Melchizedek's family origin or about his death, he is an apt figure for an eternal priesthood. As the Letter to the Hebrews points out, Melchizedek is "without father or mother or genealogy, and has neither beginning of days nor end of life" (7:3). This eternal priesthood stands out from other priesthoods, as genealogy was often a key factor in priestly identity.

Through the hypostatic union, the humanity of Christ fully shares in his divinity, and Christ in his very being possesses an eternal priesthood. His priesthood is able to fully make atonement before God: "[He] is able for all time to save those who draw near to God through him, since he always lives to make intercession for them" (Heb 7:25).

The Letter to the Hebrews depicts Christ as the High Priest of the new covenant. The paschal mystery of Christ's passion, death, and resurrection is the new and perfect sacrifice. This sacrifice, unlike that of the Old Law, does have the power to lead a person to God, fulfilling God's promise made through the prophets: "I will put my laws into their minds, and write them on their hearts, and I will be their God, and they shall be my people" (Heb 8:10; see Jer 31:33).

As in the case of the kingly and prophetic roles, Christ does not simply fulfill the role of the priesthood. He gives the priestly office a new and higher dignity. Christ's identity as the Son of God gives the figure of the priest an eternal dimension and a new dynamism. In the Old Law, even the high priest was recognized to have sins and the obligation to make reparation for them (Lv 16:6).

The author of Hebrews describes the solemn annual moment, the Day of Atonement, in which the High Priest entered the inner tabernacle, the Holy of Holies, to offer reparation for sins. The singularity of this event contrasts with the repeated sacrifices which are offered in the outer tabernacle. The special action of the High Priest offers a figure of the much more singular sacrifice of Christ, which occurred not just once a year but once for all time (see Heb 9).

Christ's priesthood brings out the full meaning of all other priesthoods. The sacrifice of the blood of animals is just a figure for Christ's sacrifice of his own self, through the shedding of his blood (Heb 9:11). The inner sanctuary of the Old Law is just a symbol of the sanctuary of heaven (Heb 9:24). The offering of animal flesh is replaced by the action of the Spirit through which Christ offers his whole person.

In this way, Christ, true God and true man, reveals the grandeur of the priestly identity. All of us, each according to our own vocation, are called to be taken up into this eternal priesthood, so that we might become "spiritual worship," offering ourselves as "a living sacrifice, holy and acceptable to God" (Rom 12:1).

CHAPTER 5

The Mysteries of the Life of Christ and their Redemptive Efficacy

Come now, bewildered am I
By joy and sorrow joined.
If today God be born,
How can He then die?
Oh, since He is man as well,
Life in His hands will be!
In this Lamb behold,
The Son of Our Sovereign God.

—St. Teresa of Avila

A. The Redemptive Meaning Present in All of Christ's Life

In the Nicene Creed we solemnly profess that Christ came down from heaven and was born of the Virgin Mary "for us men and for our salvation." We are probably well aware of the fundamental Christian truth that Christ won our salvation through his death on the Cross. Understanding the meaning of this redemptive death will be an important subject in this work.

Still, the awareness of the value of Christ's death on the Cross should not lead us to overlook the truth that all of Christ's life forms part of the Redemption. For the early Christian writers, salvation is not solely identified with any particular moment in Christ's life. Rather, for these writers, as the American theologian

Brian E. Daley notes, "it is his very *person* itself that constitutes his saving meaning for the human race." The very fact of the Word taking on a human nature has brought about a new era, in which we can partake of the divine life.

With the fact of the Incarnation, God has intervened to change the course of human nature which had been diminished by sin. Within this perspective, so important for the Fathers of the Church, the very beginning of Christ's life already contains the seed of a renewed human nature which is freed from the chains of sin. In the reality of the Word becoming flesh, God has begun a process of transformation in which God restores human nature and fills it with his presence.

The Resurrection of Christ, therefore, is a revelation of a glory which is present in Christ from the very beginning. This glory remains, in a mysterious way, hidden and still in potential during Christ's earthly life. As we shall see, Christ's risen body exists in a new and glorious manner, filled with the Holy Spirit. Christ, before his death, has not yet achieved this resplendent state. Still, in the very act of the Incarnation, we can recognize God's desire that the entire human race participate in a transformed and glorified humanity.

As in the case of the Resurrection, Christ's offering of himself at Calvary is a key expression of the divine logic which is present in all of Christ's life. By the Son's giving of himself in the Incarnation, every gesture and word of Christ has an important role in leading us to God. As the *Catechism of the Catholic Church* states, "all Jesus did, said and suffered had for its aim restoring fallen man to his original vocation" (518). In all of Christ's life, he atones for our sin and leads the human race to communion with God.

For this reason, all of the events of Christ's life are vital to fully grasp the meaning of salvation. By taking on a truly human nature, the actions of Christ relate to all of humanity.

The *Catechism* further notes, quoting St. John Paul II, that "all Christ's riches 'are for every individual and are everybody's property'" (519). All of the events of Christ's life are not simply occurrences but *mysteries*, which reflect a profound message which God has for humankind. In this chapter, we will seek to describe the salvific meaning of some of the key events or mysteries in Christ's life prior to his passion and death.

It is not a matter of trying to compare the events of our Lord's passion and death with his miracles and other actions, as if the events of Christ's life were somehow competing with one another for importance. All of the life of Christ forms a profound unity. The central message of Christ's life is that he died for our sins and rose again. This center, the paschal mystery, contains the core message God desires to convey to mankind. The paschal mystery is founded upon the other key mystery of the Christian faith, the Incarnation of the Son of God. These two mysteries are certainly of paramount importance for understanding the mystery of Christ. At the same time, these principal mysteries are of such profound richness that their true meaning is better understood from a variety of perspectives.

To appreciate a beautiful sculpture, for example, we might need to look at it from various vantage points. To use that imperfect comparison, in a similar way the different mysteries of Christ's life help us to understand the core message of Christ from various points of view. Through the many events of Christ's life, we come to understand more deeply the meaning of the Incarnation, as well as the salvation which Jesus would definitively accomplish on the Cross.

B. The Infancy and Hidden Life of Jesus

"Jesus was born in a humble stable, into a poor family . . . [I]n this poverty heaven's glory was made manifest" (*Catechism*, 525).

With his conception in the womb of the Blessed Virgin and with his birth, Christ shows that he truly has taken on a human nature.

The Fathers of the Church struggled vigorously to defend this truth, because they realized that through Christ's human nature, all of humanity is raised to a new level. As St. Athanasius succinctly pointed out, Christ "was made man that we might be made God." Through the deep solidarity which characterizes the whole human race, the fact of the Incarnation of Christ raises all human persons to a greater dignity. Through the mystery of the Incarnation, as Vatican II's Constitution *Gaudium et Spes* affirmed in memorable words, Christ "fully reveals man to man himself and makes his supreme calling clear."

All of the circumstances surrounding Christ's conception and birth manifest the same humble obedience which Christ would later show in a singular way on the Cross. St. Paul states, in his Letter to the Philippians, that Christ first empties himself by "being born in the likeness of men." He then manifests the same attitude of humility in that he "became obedient unto death, even death on a cross," and in this manner he became the source of salvation for all (Phil 2:7–8).

The Gospels show that the Word takes on flesh, in the womb of the Blessed Virgin, by a special action of the Holy Spirit. With this action, the Holy Spirit is poured out upon Our Lady in a way which had been foretold by the prophets (see Ez 36:26; Jl 2:29). The archangel Gabriel announces to Mary, at the moment of the Incarnation, that "[t]he Holy Spirit will come upon you, and the power of the Most High will overshadow you; therefore the child to be born will be called holy, the Son of God" (Lk 1:35).

These words of St. Luke's Gospel make allusion to the cloud which covered the Old Testament tent of meeting, where the tabernacle was present. Thus, at the moment of the Incarnation, Mary becomes—as the Spanish theologian Cándido Pozo noted—the "new tabernacle" in which God is especially present. The scriptural expression "holy, the Son of God" additionally emphasizes Christ's divinity, as it indicates him to be the son of God in a singular way.

The salvific meaning of the Son of God's coming into the world appears more explicitly in the angel's announcement of Christ's birth to Joseph: "Joseph, son of David, do not fear to take Mary your wife, for that which is conceived in her is of the Holy Spirit; she will bear a son, and you shall call his name Jesus, for he will save his people from their sins" (Mt 1:20–21). In the accounts of Christ's conception in the Gospels of both Luke and Matthew, the action of the Holy Spirit indicates that with the Incarnation of Christ, God's saving presence among his people has begun.

With Christ's birth in Bethlehem, the glory of God's presence now becomes visible to mankind. The humanity of the Second Person of the Trinity does not show itself to the world in great splendor. Christ is born in a manger, "because there was no place for them in the inn" (Lk 2:7). The poverty which marks Christ's life, in this moment and afterwards, shows how Christ, "though he was in the form of God, did not count equality with God a thing to be grasped, but emptied himself, taking the form of a servant, being born in the likeness of men." (Phil 2:6–7).

Here, we can see how the very beginning of Christ's earthly life is also the start of the redemptive sacrifice which would later come to its culmination at Calvary. The very fact of taking on human flesh manifests the essence of the redemptive act of Christ. The essence of the Redemption is Christ's offering of his humanity for the salvation of humankind, out of love. From this perspective we can appreciate how Christ's birth, along with his whole life, forms a profound unity with his sacrifice on the Cross.

God reveals his glory precisely in the midst of the humble circumstances of Jesus' birth. An angel of the Lord appears to shepherds in the fields nearby. "The glory of the Lord shone around them" (Lk 2:9), and the angel announces that a Savior has been born in the city of David. With the *Epiphany* or "manifestation" of Christ, Jesus reveals his splendor to wise men from the East (Mt 2:1–12). This event shows that Christ's saving mission, from its very beginning, is intended not just for the Chosen People but for all of humanity.

Christ appears in this moment as not just the fulfillment of the Hebrew Scriptures. He is also the culmination of the religious and philosophical knowledge of the Magi, and more broadly he is the definitive answer to mankind's search for truth. For all the imperfections which the knowledge of the Magi had, their learning led them to seek out the fullness of truth in Christ. For this reason, the Epiphany reminds us of the mystery of Christ, but also of the human *desire* for salvation to which this mystery responds. Joseph Ratzinger, the German theologian who served as Pope Benedict XVI, comments that this Gospel scene shows how "the inner aspiration of the human spirit, the dynamism of religions and human reason," looks for and finds fulfillment in the mystery of the Word-made-flesh.

The glory of Christ's humanity does not diminish the reality of his human nature. The infancy narratives in the Gospels make it clear that Christ, while reflecting the radiance of God, has fully identified himself with human nature in all its manifestations. Christ is born within a human genealogy, undergoes the normal period of gestation in the womb of his mother, and requires the care of this mother who "wrapped him in cloths and laid him in a manger" (Lk 2:7). With his *circumcision* and *presentation* in the temple, Jesus shows his belonging to the Chosen People and his submission to the Law.

Jesus assumes all of these realities as true man, and as true God he *transforms* these human realities and makes them a path of salvation. He is "born of woman, born under the law," precisely in order "to redeem those who were under the law, so that we might receive adoption as sons" (Gal 4:4–5). In all of these circumstances of Christ's life, his redemptive suffering continues to be present. While Christ does not have sin, he takes on the human condition of which suffering is an essential part. In his submission to the Law, he commits himself to the weighty burden of following the many precepts which the Chosen People were obliged to follow. Jesus' *flight into Egypt*, to escape the persecution of Herod, foreshadows the later opposition which Christ would face in his passion and death.

According to the will of the Father, Christ's suffering in these instances is also connected with the revelation of his glory. Christ's submission to the Law manifests the splendor of his divinity, just as this glory was also manifest in his birth. At the moment of the circumcision, Christ is given the name "Jesus," (Lk 2:21; Mt 1:21)—the Hebrew name *Yehoshu'a* — which means "God saves." After his submission to the Jewish rite of Presentation, in which Jesus is consecrated to God, Simeon is moved by the Holy Spirit to acclaim the child as "a light for revelation to the Gentiles, and for glory to thy people Israel" (Lk 2:32).

In these scenes, we can appreciate how the mysteries of Christ's infancy are the beginning of the redemptive obedience through which Christ atones for our sins. In addition, these events also begin to reveal the path which we must follow to receive the graces of salvation. Christ's childhood is a tangible lesson about the childlike disposition which we must have to enter the kingdom of God (see Mt 18:3–4). His circumcision foreshadows the sacrament of baptism, by which Christians are initiated into the new People of God.

With these revelations at the beginning of Jesus' life, the Evangelists imply that all of the moments in the life of Christ's humanity are moments which reflect the resplendence of God the Father. Each of these circumstances manifests Christ's redemptive sacrifice of himself and is illuminated by the Resurrection. As St. John affirms, to behold the mystery of the Word-made-flesh is to behold "his glory, glory as of the only Son from the Father" (Jn 1:14). At the same time, all of these moments shed light on the definitive meaning of human life.

The salvific significance of Christ's life applies in a particular way to those years which Christ spent in Nazareth, in obedience to Joseph and Mary. Because we know so little about this period, it is known as Jesus' "hidden life." For many people, these years can seem to be a period apart from Christ's salvific mission. We might be tempted to conclude that Christ began his mission of salvation when he began preaching and that he accomplished this salvation with his passion, death, and resurrection.

Without neglecting the significance of these later events, our awareness of Christ's identity leads us to appreciate that all of the years of Christ's life have a vital significance for our salvation. With his hidden life, Christ expresses more deeply the true significance of the Incarnation. He shows that the Word has truly assumed a human nature and all the ordinary realties of human life: "a daily life spent without evident greatness, a life of manual labor" (*Catechism*, 531).

As St. Josemaría Escrivá comments, "the fact that Jesus grew up and lived just like us shows us that human existence and all the ordinary activity of men have a divine meaning." Escrivá points out that the crowds would later marvel with surprise at Jesus' teaching to the masses. They were astounded because Christ was not someone out of the ordinary. While being a normal person and "the carpenter, the son of Mary" (Mk 6:3), at the same time, as Escrivá continues, "he was God; he was achieving the redemption of mankind and 'drawing all things to himself'" (see Jn 12:32)."

Here, St. Josemaría recalls Christ's prediction that he would draw all men to himself through his death on the cross (see Jn

12:32–33). The association between Christ's hidden life and this prediction implies that Jesus' ordinary life in Nazareth is part of the redemptive sacrifice of the Cross. During these years, Christ lives in obedience to the Father's will and already begins the work of undoing the disobedience of Adam. Though without sin, he accepts the toil and suffering which are associated with work as a consequence of the first sin (see Gn 3:19). Moreover, during these years Christ shows that all the customary realities of human life can be, for ordinary Christians, a way of carrying out the will of the Father and spreading the fruits of Christ's redemption.

C. The Public Life of Jesus

As we have seen, the mysteries of the infancy and hidden life of Christ give witness to the splendor of God present within the humanity of Jesus. However, the witnesses to this glory are few: Mary and Joseph, the shepherds, wise men from the East, Simeon and Anna. The manifestations of Christ's identity to these persons are a preparation for a much greater revelation still to come.

With his *public ministry*, Christ begins a broader announcement of the salvation which the Father offers through him. Jesus does so by proclaiming the coming of the kingdom of God and showing himself to be the Messiah. Through his teaching and miracles, Christ reveals the presence of God's saving power. At the same time, the public ministry is also a period of preparation for God's definitive salvation which would come about through Christ's passion, death, and resurrection. Through these final events of our Lord's time on earth, known as the *paschal mystery*, Jesus would bring about the kingdom of God and reveal the depths of God's love for us.

The *baptism* of Jesus in the River Jordan marks the opening of Christ's public life. The descent of the Spirit in the form of a dove, as well as the voice of the Father coming from heaven, announce Christ to be the Messiah and Son of God (Mt 3:16–17). This event also shows Christ to be fully identified with mankind. Jesus accepts the baptism of repentance offered by John the Baptist, and in doing so Christ demonstrates his solidarity with sinners. Jesus undergoes the baptism of John so as to redeem the human race from sin. Christ's baptism by John anticipates the true baptism which alone is able to take away sin: this "baptism" is not a purification by water, but Christ's own passion and death (see Mk 10:38).

In the ancient mindset, immersion in water was a symbol of death, for example in the destructive power of an ocean flood. At the same time, water was also recognized to be an essential source of life. In light of Christ's later death and resurrection, the early Christians would come to see the connection between this imagery of death and life. They came to see that in Christ's public ministry, as Joseph Ratzinger notes,

> his inaugural gesture is an anticipation of the Cross. . . . The baptism is an acceptance of death for the sins of humanity, and the voice that calls out "This is my beloved Son" over the baptismal waters is an anticipatory reference to the Resurrection.

The Fathers of the Church saw Christ's baptism within the framework of the anointing which would be received by kings upon taking office. This anointing is signified by the ritual of baptism, and manifested in the descent of the Spirit upon Christ. Christ's humanity is filled with the Spirit from the moment of his conception. The baptism of Jesus publicly reveals the presence of this Spirit, in fulfillment of the words of the prophet Isaiah: "The Spirit of the Lord GOD is upon me, because the LORD has anointed me to bring good tidings to the afflicted." (Is 61:1).

With this anointing, Christ shows himself to be the promised Messiah who brings salvation, but also reveals the royal identity to which all persons are called. St. Ambrose states that Christ is baptized "to purify the waters so that, washed by the flesh of Christ who did not know sin, they had the power to baptize." Christ's baptism manifests the profound transformation which occurs in the sacrament of baptism, in which "the Christian is sacramentally assimilated to Jesus" (*Catechism*, 537). Through the immersion in water, the newly baptized Christian participates in Christ's death and resurrection and comes to share in the priestly, prophetic, and kingly identity of Christ.

The *temptations* of Christ immediately follow his baptism (Lk 4:1–13). As the *Catechism* states, "the evangelists indicate the salvific meaning of this mysterious event: Jesus is the new Adam who remained faithful just where the first Adam had given into temptation" (538). Through Christ's victory over the three temptations, Christ undoes the threefold attraction of sin as found in the Book of Genesis. Scripture scholars have identified the serpent's temptation with the "the lust of the flesh and the lust of the eyes and the pride of life" which St. John describes in chapter two of his First Letter (verse 16).

When Jesus renounces the temptation to turn stones into bread, refuses the glory of "kingdoms of the world," and rejects the temptation to test God by throwing himself from the pinnacle of the temple, Jesus triumphs over the allurements to which Adam and Eve fell prey. In contrast to Adam and Eve's desire to be like god (Gn 3:5), Christ reveals the path of humble and prayerful obedience through which we can overcome sin.

Christ's victory in temptation is a prelude to his victory on the Cross. St. Luke in fact makes it clear that the devil will return at the time of Christ's passion (4:13). In this circumstance, we can see how the temptations point to recurring enticements which would diminish the true meaning of salvation. These temptations, fundamentally, would lead Christ to disobey the will of the Father so as to seek his own fulfillment. In the first temptation, the devil tempts Christ to give priority to material needs over spiritual ones. The second temptation, following the order given by St. Luke, is to seek a worldly political kingdom rather than the kingdom of God. The third temptation would demand of God an extraordinary sign.

These are temptations which Christ might have faced over the course of his life, and which have continued to face the Church down through the centuries. In a sense, all the temptations can be summarized in the challenge made to Jesus on the Cross: "And those who passed by derided him, wagging their heads and saying, 'You who would destroy the temple and build it in three days, save yourself! If you are the Son of God, come down from the cross'" (Mt 27:39–40). Instead of "saving himself," Christ's entire life—and especially his death on the Cross—shows that salvation comes from obedience to the will of the Father and from the renunciation of an exclusively worldly triumph. From the perspective of these temptations on the Cross, we can appreciate how Christ's decisive rejection of the temptations in the desert foreshadows his salvific obedience at Calvary.

With the power of the Spirit which is revealed at his baptism, and his victory over the devil's temptations, Christ inaugurates his public ministry to the Chosen People. With his *preaching*, he reveals the love of the Father toward us in a new way. God had been mentioned as father in an indirect way in the Old Testament, but in the New Testament there is a radical step forward in describing the mercy of the Father and his closeness to us. Through this new intimacy, the long-awaited kingdom of God has begun its presence in the world. We are called to respond to God's invitation with a true conversion of heart and a commitment which goes beyond the fulfillment of the Law (see Mt 5).

The *miracles* of Christ accompany his words and demonstrate that the messianic times have come. Isaiah had foretold that the coming of God's salvation would be marked by signs of healing: "[T]he eyes of the blind shall be opened, and the ears of the deaf unstopped; then shall the lame man leap like a hart, and the tongue of the dumb sing for joy" (Is 35:5–6). Still, Christ intends that the miracles serve as a sign of the deeper interior transformation which he desires to work in souls.

The original sense of the words which refer to "miracle," from the Greek root *thávma*, expresses a sense of wonder or astonishment. The miracles recounted in the Gospels are meant to arouse wonder about Christ, so as to lead to faith and salvation. However, if we are not disposed to conversion this wonder might not lead to faith. In this case, our hardness of heart can lead to another kind of astonishment. Jesus marvels at the faith of the centurion (Lk 7:9) but also at the unbelief he encounters in Nazareth (Mk 6:6).

These various reactions show that there is need for a personal response so as to be able to receive the saving power offered by Christ. The public ministry announces a salvation which has taken on a visible dimension in the person of Christ. Still, we must let ourselves become poor in spirit and humble of heart, after the example of the Lord, so as to receive this gift of God (see Mt 5:3, 11:29).

Finally, Christ's *transfiguration* offers another prelude to the Cross as well as a foretaste of the Resurrection (Mt 17:1–9). The scene recalls the great revelations of God on a mountain to Moses and Elijah (Ex 19:9; 24:15–18; 1 Kgs 19:8–18). In the intimacy of prayer with the apostles Peter, James, and John, Christ's glorious appearance reveals him to be the Messiah and Son of God. This moment shows the fulfillment of various Old Testament prophecies. The words from the bright cloud— "This is my beloved Son, with whom I am well pleased; listen to him"— recall three separate prophetic images: the Servant of Yahweh who is the object of God's special favor (Is 42:1), the

Messiah who is the Son of God (Ps 2:7), and the prophet fore-told by Moses to whom the people must listen (Dt 18:15).

The glory revealed by Christ in this scene is the glory to which each Christian is called. St. Thomas Aquinas says that while Christ's baptism proclaims the first regeneration which takes place in the sacrament of baptism, the Transfiguration manifests the mystery of the second regeneration, or the resur-rection of the elect. In this resurrection, the elect will partake in the splendor of God and the liberation from evil which are signified by the radiance of the Transfiguration. In late Jew-ish thought before the time of Christ, it was thought that the blessed would experience a miraculous change of form after the resurrection.

Even in the present life, Christians already experience this transformation through the action of grace. As St. Paul states, "[W]e all, with unveiled face, beholding the glory of the Lord, are being changed into his likeness from one degree of glory to another" (2 Cor 3:18).

While the Transfiguration foreshadows the glory of Christ's resurrection and the resurrection of the elect, it also offers a powerful reminder that this glory passes through the Cross. St. Matthew situates the scene in the context of Christ's prediction of his own suffering and death, and Peter's resistance to this mes-sage (Mt 17:21–22). St. Luke's account of the episode recounts that our Lord speaks with Moses and Elijah about "his departure, which he was to accomplish at Jerusalem" (Lk 9:31), another reference to Christ's passion. St. Mark recounts that upon com-ing down from the mountain after the Transfiguration, Christ explains that the Son of Man "should suffer many things and be treated with contempt" (Mk 9:12).

Through this mingling of heavenly glory with the remind-ers of Christ's future suffering, Jesus prepares his apostles for the salvific message which, though foretold by the prophets, was so radically novel to the Jewish mind. This message is that the long-awaited and exalted Messiah would open the way to salvation by means of suffering and humiliation. He has come to manifest the glory which Israel had long awaited: as Joseph Ratzinger comments, "a glory, however, that forever bears the mark of Jesus' wounds."

CHAPTER 6

The Sacrifice of the Cross

The cross is the way which leads from earth to heaven.
Those who embrace it with faith, love, and hope are taken
up, right into the heart of the Trinity.

                                    —*St. Teresa Benedicta of the Cross*

The opening of St. John's account of the Last Supper expresses
the extraordinary meaning of the last moments of Christ's life:
"[W]hen Jesus knew that his hour had come to depart out of
this world to the Father, having loved his own who were in
the world, he loved them to the end" (13:1). This period is a
supreme manifestation of the charity which motivated Jesus'
entire life. These moments cast a new and definitive light on the
extent of God's love for us and the profound reality of salvation.
This chapter and the next will examine the salvific meaning of
Christ's passion and death on the Cross.

A. The Predictions of Christ regarding his Death: The Last Supper and the Meaning of the Passion

At the moment of Christ's entry into the temple, in the Presentation, Simeon foretells the opposition which Jesus' mission
would encounter (Lk 2:34–35). Christ shows an awareness of
this future from the beginning of his public life. As he comes to
his own town of Nazareth, he recognizes that "[a] prophet is not

without honor, except in his own country, and among his own
kin, and in his own house" (Mk 6:4).

Throughout his ministry, Christ demonstrates an awareness
that his suffering and death is the Father's will (see, for example, Mt 20:22, Lk 13:32, and Jn 6:51). As God, Jesus would have
had perfect knowledge of the future. Although the knowledge of
this future might conceivably have occurred in his human nature
through a meditation on the Hebrew Scriptures, Christ shows
an immediacy in his knowledge of the Father which is incom-
patible with such a process of learning. As he affirms, "All things
have been delivered to me by my Father" (Mt 11:27).

In addition to these more indirect references to Christ's
death, St. Mark records three specific passages in which Jesus
explicitly predicts his passion and death. The first one occurs
immediately after Peter's confession of Jesus as the Christ. Christ
commands strict discretion regarding his identity, and proceeds
to purify any vision of an earthly or politically victorious messiah: "[H]e began to teach them that the Son of man must suffer
many things, and be rejected by the elders and the chief priests
and the scribes, and be killed, and after three days rise again"
(Mk 8:31). The second prediction, shortly after the Transfiguration, similarly offers a more accurate portrayal of the messiah.
Christ's words correct any misunderstanding of the heavenly
vision of Christ beheld by Peter, James, and John on the mountain (Mk 9:31). Finally, on the path to Jerusalem, near Jericho,
Christ predicts his passion in detail (Mk 10:34).

The apostles, lacking the gift of the Holy Spirit, are unable to
grasp the meaning of these predictions (Mk 9:32). Still, through
these various declarations by Jesus, the Evangelists make it clear
that Christ's death forms part of God's plan. Christ's ability to
predict and interpret his own death casts an important light on
the significance of this death. This capacity makes it evident
that Jesus' death is part of the will of the Father which Christ

willingly accepts. By providing this broader and more supernatural perspective, the predictions help us to understand that his death truly brings about the Redemption, and that this death is not simply an admirable act of obedience.

The predictions of our Lord about his own death become clearer and more frequent as the moment of his parting from this world approaches. In particular, at the *Last Supper*, Christ shows an unambiguous awareness of his imminent death, as well as of the redemptive value of his self-giving. St. Matthew reveals this awareness when he recounts Christ's words over the cup: "Drink of it, all of you; for this is my blood of the covenant, which is poured out for many for the forgiveness of sins" (Mt 26:27–28). With this command, Christ not only predicts but also makes present, in an anticipated and sacramental manner, the same sacrifice which would be consummated on the Cross hours later. By instituting the sacrament of the Holy Eucharist, Jesus inaugurates the true worship in his Blood which is alone capable of taking away sins.

Luke's account most clearly explains that the rite instituted by Christ at the Last Supper is Christ's "passover" (Lk 22:15). This Passover is not the same as the Jewish rite of Passover. Christ establishes the sacrament of the Holy Eucharist in the context of the Jewish Passover meal, though it seems likely that the Crucifixion took place on the day before the Jewish Passover. In fact, the Last Supper is, as St. Luke indicates, not *the* Passover but "this Passover," that is, the Passover as it has been transformed by Christ's saving action. Jesus' death on the Cross would bring to fulfillment the saving action of God which the Jewish rite commemorated.

The other details which surround the Last Supper help to fully express the rich meaning of Christ's total self-giving on the cross. The *washing of the feet* of the disciples manifests Christ's attitude of service to us, but also of our need to let ourselves be served by Christ's action. Peter must let his feet be washed, and in this gesture we are reminded of our need to freely and humbly allow ourselves to receive the gift of salvation. Christ predicts his suffering as well as his future glorification, and promises the gift of the Holy Spirit as the fruit of his death and resurrection (Mk 14:25, Jn 16:7).

B. The Circumstances of the Passion of Christ

All of the Evangelists narrate Christ's passion with the awareness that Jesus shows his divine identity precisely within these moments of the deepest humiliation and suffering. While each Gospel recounts the Passion with a particular emphasis, the key elements are clear.

Jesus' proclamation of the kingdom of God was viewed as a threat to the Law as well as the power of the religious authorities. He seemed to be acting against some of the fundamental principles of the Chosen People. He claimed to authoritatively interpret the Law, one of the most cherished institutions in Israel, but in doing so he was seen to go against the fulfillment of the Law. Christ was accused of similarly lacking in veneration for the temple, the special site of God's presence in the Old Testament (Mk 14:57–58). Jesus' claim to forgive sins, an action which only God can carry out, was a particular source of scandal (Lk 5:21).

Accepting the message of Christ's teaching requires a radical conversion of heart and mind, under the influence of divine grace. For the Chosen People at Jesus' time, this conversion meant confiding in Christ's authority rather than the conventional interpretations of the Law. Most of the religious authorities of the time were unwilling to accept such a change of outlook. In this refusal lies the root of the tragic condemnation of Jesus to death.

Jesus' raising of Lazarus from the dead, in the midst of an atmosphere of fierce opposition to him on the part of the leading religious authorities, marks a decisive moment which leads to Christ's death. This miracle is the culmination of the great signs worked by Jesus during his public ministry, as described in the Gospel of John. Lazarus' resurrection offers a particular sign of the final resurrection as well as the believer's rising from sin to a state of grace. In the face of this and the other signs of Jesus, the chief priests and Pharisees respond: "What are we to do? For this man performs many signs. If we let him go on thus, everyone will believe in him, and the Romans will come and destroy both our holy place and our nation" (Jn 11: 47–48). Here, we can see how the leaders saw Jesus' preaching as a pressing threat to Israel's very identity as a nation.

Jesus in fact showed the greatest respect for the Law and the temple. At the same time, he came to bring these realities to fulfillment through his own person. In the New Law and new temple realized in Christ, the political and religious kingdom of Israel would give way to a new and universal kingdom of God which was distinct from any kind of political rule. This radical detachment of the kingdom of God from an earthly kingdom could only come about by means of Christ's Cross. As Joseph Ratzinger observes, "only through the total loss of all external power, through the radical stripping away that led to the Cross, could this new world come into being."

In the face of the dilemma created by Lazarus' resurrection, Caiaphas unwittingly gives voice to this divine "necessity" of the Cross: "[Y]ou do not understand that it is expedient for you that one man should die for the people, and that the whole nation should not perish" (Jn 11:50). This advice follows from his prophecy earlier that year, as high priest, that "Jesus should die for the nation, and not for the nation only, but to gather into one the children of God who are scattered abroad" (Jn 11:51–52). These words would have originally referred to the Jewish hope that the People of Israel, scattered across the world, would be gathered together again in their homeland.

In this way, Caiaphas expresses the hope that the death of Jesus will bring the Jewish people together as a nation. The prophecy in this sense would prove to be false, in view of the Roman destruction of Jerusalem and the temple in AD 70. However, in light of Christ, the prophecy expresses a deeper truth. Jesus' death would precisely bring about a new People of God whose boundaries go beyond that of any nation. The national unity desired by the Jewish leaders would give way to a spiritual unity rooted in Christ's definitive sacrifice.

Caiaphas' words, in the limited way in which his hearers would have understood them, convince the chief priests and Pharisees to eliminate Jesus: "So from that day on they took counsel how to put him to death" (Jn 11:53).

The Evangelists recount the trial of Jesus in two distinct stages. After the betrayal by Judas, Jesus is first led at night before the high priest, where "all the chief priests and the elders and the scribes were assembled" (Mk 14:53). This group of religious leaders, known as the Sanhedrin, was the highest Jewish court of justice. It dealt with religious, legal, and civic matters related to the Jewish people.

The first stage of the trial seems to have been a cross-examination of Jesus. The first charge made against Jesus has to do with the temple: "[T]wo came forward and said, 'This fellow said, "I am able to destroy the temple of God, and to build it in three days"'" (Mt 26:61). The high priest asks Jesus to answer for the charge, and Christ responds by silence. This charge does not seem to have been enough to lead to the death sentence sought by the accusers.

The second charge to which Jesus must answer concerns his identity as the Messiah, a figure also known as the Christ: "Are you the Christ, the Son of the Blessed?" (Mk 14:61). The Gospels of Matthew, Mark, and Luke report slightly different versions of Christ's response, but in each account Jesus is clearly understood to have responded in the affirmative. The high priest tears his garments as a sign of Christ's blasphemy, and the rest of the Sanhedrin concurs with Caiaphas' opinion.

The charge of blasphemy is due not simply to the fact of Jesus' claim to be the Messiah, but rather is the result of his assertion of being equal to God: "[Y]ou will see the Son of man sitting at the right hand of Power, and coming with the clouds of heaven" (Mk 14:62). This role of the messiah was foretold in the Scriptures (Ps 110:5, Dn 7:13). Still, Christ fulfilled these prophecies in a way which was completely unexpected for the Jewish leaders.

The members of the Sanhedrin are unable to change their outlook. They cannot accept that Christ is the figure whom they had expected to be so majestic and politically triumphant, nor can they appreciate the deeper spiritual meaning of the messiah. It is significant to note that it has never been clear why Jesus' words would actually be a blasphemy in the Jewish law. The claim to be the messiah, even if it were false, was not considered to be such an offense. The sentence against Jesus manifests the spiritual blindness of the members of the Sanhedrin rather than any actual transgression on the part of Christ.

The Sanhedrin finds Jesus worthy of the death sentence. As the Romans have the authority to execute this penalty, Christ is bound and accused in the court of the Roman governor, Pontius Pilate. Whereas the Sanhedrin charged Christ with blasphemy, before the governor Christ's accusers emphasize the political dimension: "We found this man perverting our nation, and forbidding us to give tribute to Caesar, and saying that he himself is Christ a king" (Lk 23:2).

The charge of claiming to be king of the Jews is a charge of treason against the Roman authority, and would be deserving of death. However, Pilate at first does not give importance to the accusation. The elders and chief priests use a political maneuver to get him to change his mind. They threaten to denounce him for supporting an enemy of the emperor: "If you release this man, you are not Caesar's friend; everyone who makes himself a king sets himself against Caesar" (Jn 19:12). Such tactics were common in Israel at the time.

In addition to the leading Jewish and Roman authorities, the Evangelists also identify a "crowd" of persons who clamor for Christ's death (Mt 27:15). This crowd would not have gathered for Jesus' trial but rather for the amnesty which the governor offered on the occasion of the Passover (Mt 27:15). The chief priests and the elders convince the multitude to ask for the release of Barabbas, a man who has committed murder in an insurrection (Mk 15:7). The crowd, like the religious leaders, has been deceived by the vision of an earthly and political messiah. They cry out for Christ to receive crucifixion, a common capital punishment for slaves and non-Jews. "So Pilate, wishing to satisfy the crowd, released for them Barabbas; and having scourged Jesus, he delivered him to be crucified" (Mk 15:15).

C. The Causes of the Passion and Death of Christ

The Gospel accounts reveal that a multitude of factors led to Christ's death. The Roman soldiers execute the sentence of death. They do so at the command of the Roman governor. The governor, in turns, acts under intense pressure from a crowd and in particular at the urging of the chief priests, scribes, and Pharisees. St. Mark comments that the chief priests deliver up Jesus out of "envy" (15:10). As noted, these leaders lack the proper dispositions needed to appreciate the true meaning of the Scriptures and of Christ's mission. They saw Jesus as a threat to the Jewish institutions which they held so dearly: the Law, the temple, and national unity. As the *Catechism of the Catholic Church* points out, the Sanhedrin acts "at the same time out of 'ignorance' and the 'hardness' of their 'unbelief'" (591; see Lk 23:34; Acts 3:17–18; Mk 3:5; and Rom 11:25, 20).

However, those responsible for Jesus' death cannot be limited to a specific group of Romans or Jews. One of the apostles, Judas, takes the initiative to hand over Jesus to the chief priests (Mt 26:14–15). St. John comments that this apostle, though specially chosen by Christ, is a thief and has become blinded to the teachings of the Lord (Jn 12:5–6).

The Gospels recognize that the various betrayals of Jesus have a still deeper cause: the devil. St. John's Gospel identifies the devil as the one who inspires Judas to betray Christ (Jn 13:2). Upon being arrested, Christ recognizes his imminent passion and death is a time belonging to "the power of darkness" (Lk 22:53). In fact, as noted in the last chapter, the misunderstandings which led to Christ's death correspond to the temptations which the devil makes to Christ in the desert. Many of the Chosen People are unfortunately led astray by the temptation to prioritize earthly and political considerations. These are the same considerations to which the devil gives priority in the desert: the temptation to turn stone into bread, to idolize the "kingdoms of the world," and to make an extraordinary show of God's power (see Lk 4:3–11).

These indications of the Gospels with regard to the devil's action reveal that the origin of Christ's tragic fate is not simply the result of the persons who were most immediately involved. The deepest origin of Christ's passion is to be found in the same creature, Satan, who led the first man and woman into sin. This first sin has placed all of humanity into a state of enmity with God (see Rom 5:12). This presence of sin in the world explains the hatred of the world toward the disciples of Christ (see Jn 15:18–19). In each and every sin, we follow the same path of spiritual blindness and malice which the persecutors of Christ show in seeking his death. In each sin, we follow the temptation of the devil and seeks out a lesser good in the place of God.

From this vantage point, we can understand how the sins of *all* humanity are the deepest cause of Christ's passion. The *Catechism of the Catholic Church*, quoting the *Roman Catechism* of the sixteenth century, states: "In her Magisterial teaching of the faith and in the witness of her saints, the Church has never forgotten that 'sinners were the authors and the ministers of all the sufferings that the divine Redeemer endured.'" The sin of those who were the specific historical protagonists in Christ's death, as the twentieth-century Spanish theologian Manuel González-Gil observes, "are no more than a summary and crystallization of all the sins of men."

Christ's tragic passion and death manifest, in a new and definitive light, the extent of the evil which is present in sin. The final moments of Jesus' life allow us, through the lens of faith, to appreciate the offense against God which has been present from the beginning of human history, and which will sadly continue until the end of time.

D. The Initiative of the Father and the "Abandonment" of Jesus

While Christ's suffering and death manifest the reality of evil in a most intense way, the Evangelists are also careful to note that God's plan is not defeated by this malice. At Pentecost, St. Peter announces that Jesus was "delivered up according to the definite plan and foreknowledge of God" (Acts 2:23). The existence of such a design is made clear though Christ's predictions of his own death, as well as the various Old Testament prophecies that foretell the sufferings of the messiah.

How could God will that his Son should suffer such a cruel fate? Theologians, or anyone for that matter, have not had an easy time understanding this. Certainly, God did not inspire the chief priests and Roman authorities to put Christ to death, although by his perfect knowledge God knew this would happen. What God the Father has fundamentally willed is to send his Son into the world, so as to lead us to a new participation in the divine life (see Gal 4:4–5). We freely rejected this divine intention, due to our own free choice of sin. Still, God willed to accept this rejection. This will of God to assent to the Passion does not mean that God the Father somehow would derive pleasure from Christ's suffering. Rather, the Father willed Christ's death because it would bring about redemption for sins and offer the greatest manifestation of God's love for us.

The New Testament describes this will of the Father as an act of love, but also as a *command*. As he prepares for his passion and death, Jesus tells the apostles: "I do as the Father has commanded me" (Jn 14:31). God willed the passion and death of Christ for the salvation of the human race, and so Christ's suffering and death are a real act of *obedience*. As St. Paul affirms, Christ "became obedient unto death, even death on a cross" (Phil 2:8). Christ's obedience is an essential part of the Redemption. His death manifests obedience in its maximum realization, and this submission undoes the disobedience of man's first sin (see Rom 5:19).

The great mysteries of both the Father's will and Christ's humble obedience reveal themselves in a special way in the last moments of Christ's life. The Son of God's humiliation reaches the point in which he seems to be "abandoned" by God:

> And when the sixth hour had come, there was darkness over the whole land until the ninth hour. And at the ninth hour Jesus cried with a loud voice, "*Elo-i, Elo-i, lama sabach-thani?*" which means, "My God, my God, why hast thou forsaken me?"

(Mk 15:33–34). The bystanders still look for an extraordinary sign of Christ's messianic identity: "'Wait, let us see whether Elijah will come to take him down'" (15:36). However, no such sign arrives before Christ's death: "And Jesus uttered a loud cry, and breathed his last" (15:37).

Some have interpreted these final words as indicating a spiritual desolation in which Christ was actually abandoned by the Father. Jesus would supposedly experience such a state so as to offer a consolation to those who experience interior trials. Certainly, Christ's suffering does offer hope in the face of the many different afflictions which affect human life. Christ's cry shows the extent to which he truly has taken on a human condition and identified himself with the sufferings of all mankind. Joseph Ratzinger notes that

> Jesus is praying the great psalm of suffering Israel, and so he is taking upon himself all the tribulation, not just of Israel, but of all those in this world who suffer from God's concealment. He brings the world's anguished cry at God's absence before the heart of God himself.

Even so, the idea of Christ being abandoned by God is not consistent with the divine identity of Christ as shown in the Gospels. All of Jesus' actions reflect the fact that he and the Father "are one" (Jn 10:30). Christ's plea on the Cross takes up the words of Psalm 22 (verse 1). This psalm expresses the sorrow of an apparent abandonment in the face of persecution, but also a confident hope in God's help.

The psalm prophetically foretells the sufferings of Christ, including the mockery of bystanders as well as the casting of lots for Jesus' clothing. But the psalm ends with the assurance that God "has not despised or abhorred the affliction of the afflicted; and he has not hid his face from him, but has heard, when he cried to him" (Ps 22:24). As in the case of the Suffering Servant found in the Book of Isaiah, the fruits of the psalmist's agony are foretold: "All the ends of the earth shall remember and turn to the LORD; and all the families of the nations shall worship before him" (Ps 22:27). Christ's sorrowful cry is therefore also a petition of hope which looks trustingly to the salvation of all humanity, a salvation which is precisely being accomplished on the Cross.

E. The Glory of the Cross

In his passion and death, Christ takes on the greatest of human affliction, and through his divine nature he transforms this pain. Through his love and obedience, the Cross becomes the preeminent sign of Christ's triumph. The last of the Gospels to be written, that of St. John, has a particular awareness of the glory or splendor of God which is revealed through the Cross. The Evangelist describes Christ's suffering as an elevation: "[A]s Moses lifted up the serpent in the wilderness, so must the Son of man be lifted up, that whoever believes in him may have eternal life" (Jn 3:14–15). For St. John this verb, "to be lifted up" or "to be raised up," has a double meaning. The expression refers to Christ's being elevated at the moment of his crucifixion, but also to his being "raised up" by his resurrection and ascension.

At the moments of his most extreme agony and even in his dead body, Christ's humanity continues to reveal the glory of God. The reality of his dead body coexists alongside his identity as Lord of life and death. Christ shows his power in the very offering up of his own life: "No one takes it from me, but I lay it down of my own accord. I have power to lay it down, and I have power to take it again" (Jn 10:18).

The Cross is glorious because it reveals, in the utmost way, the splendor of God's holiness, which has led him to offer himself completely for the life of men. It is the supreme act of worship, through which Christ offers himself and all creation to the glory of the Father. God calls all humanity to recognize this glory and respond in adoration like the centurion: "Truly this man was the Son of God!" (Mk 15:39).

CHAPTER 7

The Redemptive Value of the Sacrifice of Christ (I)

Why did Christ die on a Cross? Was this horrible Passion necessary to free us from our inner darkness? Certainly not. God could have forgiven our sins in a thousand different ways, or simply not at all. Our Lord probably chose the most impressive way of all, the one that most clearly manifests the madness of his great love.

—*Jutta Burggraf, German theologian, 1952–2010*

A. The Merit of the Sufferings and Death of Christ

Merit is a fairly common concept in human life. We might say, for example, that a worker merits a promotion because he has accomplished a set of specific goals in his job. With this, we mean to say that because of our effort, we have a certain right to a given reward. We could probably think of many other examples from everyday life.

As familiar as the concept might sound, the idea of applying merit to God can seem awkward. This impression is correct: strictly speaking we do not have the right to demand anything of God. Otherwise, God would not be the fullness of good; he would be required to do something for us.

The case is far different in the case of Christ, true God and true man. Because his actions are truly actions of God, Christ can merit in the strict sense. He does have a right to a recompense. In his case, the fitting reward is the honor and the glory which are due to God alone.

God the Son already has the fullness of this glory from all eternity. In the intimacy of his prayer at the Last Supper, Christ speaks to the Father of "the glory which I had with thee before the world was made" (Jn 17:5). However, at the same moment, Christ asks the Father to "glorify thou me in thy own presence" with this same glory which he has had all from all eternity.

Through the Incarnation, Christ is glorified not just in his being as God, but also in his *human* nature. In the mysteries of Christ's life which we have seen up to now, God reveals the glory which is present in Jesus' humanity. The angels who praise Christ at his birth recognize the splendor of God which is present in his sacred humanity. At the Baptism and the Transfiguration, the voice from a cloud, which proclaims Christ to be the unique Son of God, also pays homage to this same human aspect. The humanity of Christ receives its definitive glorification in the Resurrection and the Ascension.

In these and all of the actions of the one who is both God and man, Christ opens up the possibility of a certain human merit. Through Christ, we can say that human nature has the right to receive honor and glory. In the sixteenth century, the Council of Trent taught that Jesus Christ "merited Justification for us by His most holy Passion on the wood of the Cross."

One should not think of merit in an overly legalistic sense, as it might apply to merit in human life. A worker who does his job for one hour, for example, is entitled to a certain wage. Under the relevant conditions, a company would be required to provide such a salary to a worker. God, on the other hand, is not obligated to offer a reward to creatures.

Still, Scripture shows us clearly that God is not detached from the good and evil that his creatures carry out. "The way of the wicked is an abomination to the LORD, but he loves him who pursues righteousness" (Prv 15:9). Revelation shows us the existence of a moral order in which good actions are worthy of reward and evil actions deserve punishment.

God honors the good and abhors evil, but not because this good or evil affects him in the deepest sense. God always remains transcendent to his creation. He respects the freedom of rational creatures, both angels and humans. Nonetheless, he is also the infinitely just Creator and ruler of the universe, and guides the world according to his providence. He wants human beings and all creatures to conform to this design, for their true good and to manifest his glory. God's reward and punishment are ordered to this plan.

The actions of Christ realize the good in a singular way. When we say that the deeds of the Son of God are worthy of merit, we are saying that Jesus' actions as God and as man are fully pleasing in the eyes of God and deserving of honor. At the Baptism and the Transfiguration, God the Father proclaims that he is "well pleased" with Christ (Mt 3:17; 17:5). St. Paul indicates that as a result of Christ's humble obedience, Jesus is definitively glorified by the Father (see Phil 2:8–9).

Christ's actions have merit in the fullest way, in the sense that they are deserving of glorification. Our actions can have a merit in a lesser way. Since we are creatures, all the good that we have and do comes from God. God is the only one really deserving of honor. Still, the Creator in his goodness has allowed us to attain what is called quasi-merit or *congruous* merit as a reward for our good actions. This merit is not strictly due to our actions but is fundamentally a consequence of God's loving promise to us.

B. The Notion of Satisfaction

Theologians traditionally distinguish between merit and *satisfaction* as aspects of Christ's redemptive work. While merit refers to a reward that we are entitled to, satisfaction refers to the reparation for a wrong that we have done. In reference to Christ, merit refers to the reward of eternal glory which Christ wins for us, while satisfaction refers to Christ's action of redeeming us from sin.

We tend to think of satisfaction in regard to the fulfillment of desires. If I am hungry, and then I have something to eat, I might say that I am satisfied. In the theological sense, satisfaction refers not to our desires but to those of God. God, who has the entirety of all perfections, possesses the fullness of holiness and justice. He desires goodness for the universe, and through sin we freely depart from this plan. In the final analysis, sin does harm to us and to creation. Sin does not take away from God's goodness.

Still, God is infinitely just and because of this he is rightly offended by our sin. In light of this reality, Christian tradition from Augustine onwards has distinguished between our *guilt* for sin and the *punishment* by which we make up for the disorder caused by sin.

St. Anselm of Canterbury, an Italian Benedictine monk and doctor of the church from the turn of the eleventh century, made a significant contribution to the theological concept of satisfaction. He described the offense of sin, and the need for satisfaction to atone for this disorder, in his important work *Cur Deus Homo*, from the year 1099. Anselm notes that every rational creature should be subject to God. When man sins, he therefore incurs a debt with God which must be repaid. As Anselm asserts, "He who does not render this honor which is due to God, robs God of his own and dishonors him; and this is sin." We remain in a state of sin until this offense is atoned for:

> So long as he does not restore what he has taken away, he remains in fault; and it will not suffice merely to restore what has been taken away, but, considering the contempt offered, he ought to restore more than he took away.

Some have criticized Anselm's perspective for putting too much emphasis on the legal aspect of satisfaction. Nonetheless, we can understand the offense of sin not simply in a legalistic way, but rather in terms of the requirements of God's justice. In sin, we offend the order which God has desired for creation. God reveals his holiness and justice precisely when he recognizes the evil of sin. Like a loving father who has concern for his child, God cannot remain indifferent before our choice of evil.

Due to this situation, God is just to seek *satisfaction* for sins. The root of the word (*satisfacere*) literally means "to make enough." This etymological context reminds us that, in some way, we need to adequately make up for the disorder caused by sin. In the deepest sense, this satisfaction is for our good; God does not need our atonement. Sin has disturbed the right ordering of our soul and for our good this needs to be corrected. Because of the offense to God which sin entails and also because of our sinful state due to our offense, we are not able to make adequate satisfaction by our own efforts.

The awareness of the need for satisfaction, as we have seen in the earlier chapter on redemption, is not something peculiar to Christianity. The awareness of the guilt incurred by us and the desire to atone for this guilt are present in the other world religions. These religions, the Jewish religion included, often seek to pass on guilt by transferring it to a substitute. In this way, the punishment due to sin would be passed on to the substitute so that the person or persons would be liberated from sin.

This action of being purified of sin by means of a substitute is known as *vicarious atonement*. The concept has an important role in the Old Testament. The laying of the hands of the priest upon a sacrificed animal seemed to function as way of transferring the sins of the people onto the animal (Lv 1:4). At times, the substitute is a person. Such is the case with Moses, who offers that he himself be blotted out of God's book so as to forgive the people's idolatry on Mount Sinai (Ex 32:32).

These sacrifices and those present in other religions offer an important testimony to the desire for atonement. Ultimately, however, all of these oblations fall short of their desired intention. The psalmist recognizes that "[s]acrifice and offering thou dost not desire," but God instead desires a heart which desires to do his will (Ps 40:6).

On our own, we are not capable of offering to God this rectitude of heart. St. Anselm asserts that since sin offends the majesty of God, only God himself is capable of making proper satisfaction for sin. On the other hand, we are the ones at fault for sin, so we are the ones who should make reparation. Hence, Anselm holds that one who is both God and man must make satisfaction.

We should understand this "necessity" of God to become man in the proper context. God himself did not "need" to take on a human flesh. However, we can say that we are in need of God becoming flesh for our salvation. In this context Thomas Aquinas quotes the Gospel of St. John: "The Son of man must be lifted up, that whosoever believeth in Him may not perish, but may have life everlasting" (Jn 3:14–15, Aquinas' translation). The Incarnation was necessary so that human beings might completely fulfill the requirements of God's justice and fully atone for the offenses of mankind.

C. The Passion and Death of Christ as Satisfaction

In Anselm's view, the action of Christ saves us precisely because it is gratuitous and not necessary on the part of God. Although in a sense all of Christ's action is a gratuitous gift, Anselm focuses in particular on those actions which Christ was not obligated to carry out. Christ's obedience to God's law as a man was something he was required to do as a man. However, as man he was not required to suffer grievously for the sins of others. As a result, Christ's gratuitous offering of himself, by his passion and death, is able to make satisfaction to God for the sins of mankind.

Anselm's perspective is rather juridical and would be completed by later theology. Still, his vision offers a way of understanding the Redemption which is in keeping with the mystery revealed by God. The notion that Christ died for our sins is a fundamental truth present in Sacred Scripture. The roots of this teaching are already present in the Old Testament. The idea of vicarious atonement is most fully developed in the *Suffering Servant* described in the Book of Isaiah. As we have seen in chapter three, this scriptural image is an important expression of mediation.

The Suffering Servant lacks the glorious characteristics of the messiah: "[H]e had no form or comeliness that we should look at him," and is a man "despised and rejected by men; a man of sorrows, and acquainted with grief" (53:2–3). The humiliation and sufferings of this servant are the sufferings of the people: "[H]e has borne our griefs and carried our sorrows" (53:4). These afflictions are due to sin. The Suffering Servant has taken on the punishment due to the people's sins, so as to purify these offenses: "[H]e was wounded for our transgressions, he was bruised for our iniquities; upon him was the chastisement that made us whole, and with his stripes we are healed" (53:5).

The New Testament would show that Jesus Christ fulfills this figure of the Suffering Servant. St. Peter shows Christ to be this servant when he says:

> He committed no sin; no guile was found on his lips. When he was reviled, he did not revile in return; when he suffered, he did not threaten; but he trusted to him who judges justly. He himself bore our sins in his body on the tree, that we might die to sin and live to righteousness. By his wounds you have been healed. (1 Pt 2:22–24)

Many other texts of the New Testament echo the sentiment that Christ died for sins: for example, 1 Corinthians 15:3, Romans 4:25, and Galatians 1:4. In describing the gospel message, St. Paul states that it is of "first importance" that "Christ died for our sins in accordance with the scriptures, that he was buried, that he was raised on the third day in accordance with the scriptures" (1 Cor 15:3–4).

St. Paul describes Christ, in light of this role in undoing the work of sin, as the *New Adam* (see Rom 5:12–21). St. Paul's description of the relationship between Adam and Christ sheds light on the way in which Christ's death atones for the sin of man. Both Adam and Christ manifest the opposition between "one" person and "all." Through Adam's *one* act of disobedience, a state of sin entered into the world which affects *all* humanity. This state is the state of original sin, and is distinct from the personal sins which each person commits. Still, humanity in this state is lacking in its correct relationship with God.

St. Paul insists that Adam was only a type or prefiguration of Christ. Adam's one act of disobedience, which affected all, was only a prelude to Christ's one act of obedience which brings life to all. The notion of the New Adam helps us to appreciate the solidarity by which Christ acts as a vicar or representative for all of us.

The aforementioned scriptural passages show that while satisfaction is not present in the Scriptures, the term reflects a key message of Christianity. This message is that Christ has atoned to God for the offense caused by sin. The Fathers of the Church would draw out the richness of this important idea. St. Irenaeus, bishop of Lyons and the great Christian theologian of the second century, is a prime early example. He comments that man has been able to learn the things of God and has come to be in communion with him by the fact of the Word becoming man. Irenaeus describes the redeeming action of Christ as "redeeming us by His own blood in a manner consonant to reason."

The great bishop of Lyons emphasizes, as Anselm later would, that man has been redeemed in a way which man can understand—at least to some extent—by reason. Irenaeus stresses that God's plan of redemption occurs in a manner which is in keeping with the infinite wisdom of God. God, acting with this wisdom, desires to save the human person who is his creation, and does so in a way which preserves God's perfect justice. Christ has done so "giving His soul for our souls, and His flesh for our flesh." This gift of Christ's blood, Irenaeus further notes, is accompanied by the gift of the Holy Spirit which restores our immortality.

The Fathers would describe Christ's redemption and clarify various misunderstandings which arose with regard to this mystery. They recognized that sin had brought about a deeper loss of order in the whole of being, which Christ has come to restore. Athanasius highlighted that the Redemption was not simply the removal of sin but a deeper renewal of man's nature. This perspective can help us avoid an overly legalistic approach to the Redemption. Sin is indeed an offense against God's law. Still, it is an offense against not simply a set of rules but against the fundamental order which God has inscribed within creation and in the human person.

The Fathers took care to describe how in the Redemption, Christ is sinless while at the same time, in an inscrutable way, he takes on the consequences of sin. Christ has assumed a human nature which, due to sin, is in a diminished state. Jesus has done this precisely to do away with the corruption of sin.

St. Gregory of Nanzianzus, the fourth-century archbishop of Constantinople and important teacher of the doctrine on the Trinity, rejects the claim that somehow the Redemption occurred through a negotiation between God and Satan. According to such a view, the Father would have offered the Son as a "ransom." Instead, the holy humanity of Christ, "the Humanity of God" as Gregory calls it, has in itself the power to sanctify all of humanity.

Another important early Christian writer, Tertullian, who lived at the turn of the third century, seems to have been the first person to use the word *satisfaction* in a theological sense. He was a lawyer and appears to have taken the concept from Roman law. In this legal framework, satisfaction referred to the amends made to another for the failure to fulfill an obligation. Within the same juridical perspective, St. Hilary of Poiters, the fourth-century French bishop and doctor of the church, describes Christ's suffering and death as accomplishing a "penal function" by which the curse of sin might be removed.

With time and the influence of Roman and Germanic culture, this explanation of sin in legal language would take on greater significance. The offense of sin would be understood as an offense against the lawful order over which God presides. This is the background of the notion of satisfaction described by Anselm. When Anselm asserts that God must become man in order to fully satisfy the offense of sin, he is showing that the Redemption has occurred in a way which fulfilled the strictest requirements of justice.

Thomas Aquinas would take up Anselm's explanation and place it in a fuller context. Aquinas would go beyond earlier explanations, with their emphasis on legal categories, and explain satisfaction as a mystery of *love*.

Aquinas' perspective helps us to see divine justice in a way which is focused on the *person*. As we have noted, in committing a sin, we disrupt the proper order of justice in our own souls and in his relationship with the world around us. The need for punishment, then, is fundamentally a way of restoring—within us and in the world around us—the proper harmony with God's plan. Rather than simply a legal requirement, satisfaction is a way of helping and healing the person and creation as a whole.

Aquinas—or the Angelic Doctor, as he is known—affirms that Christ's passion is an act of atonement which properly satisfies the offense of sin. He explains the reasons for the satisfaction offered by Christ: "By suffering out of love and obedience, Christ gave more to God than was required to compensate for the offense of the whole human race."

In the first place, as Aquinas notes, the atonement made by Christ's passion is due to the exceeding charity which Christ shows in his suffering. This charity more than compensates for the lack of love shown in the sins of all mankind.

Secondly, as the Angelic Doctor continues, Christ's passion makes atonement because of "the dignity of His life which He laid down in atonement, for it was the life of one who was God and man." As man, Christ is linked to all of humanity. All those who form part of the Church become one mystical body with him, with Christ as the head (see Col 1:18). Since all the faithful are members united in one body with Christ, Christ's satisfaction belongs to all the faithful. All persons, in turn, are called to be united to this Body of Christ, which is the Church.

Thirdly and finally, Aquinas observes that Christ's passion offers satisfaction for man due to "the extent of the Passion, and the greatness of the grief endured." During these moments, Christ underwent genuine pain, which he experienced within his human nature. Christ's suffering was in fact the very greatest of pain. This suffering for the sake of justice serves to repay the sins of the human race, in keeping with the words of St. Matthew which Aquinas alludes to: "Blessed are those who are persecuted for righteousness' sake" (Mt 5:10). In an unfathomable way, Christ's decision to accept his suffering, moved by his interior attitude of obedience and love, makes up for all of the offense created by the sins of mankind.

As the great Dominican notes, to truly atone for sin requires that one "offers something which the offended one loves equally, or even more than he detested the offense." God is more satisfied with the offering of Christ, made in the name of all humanity, than he is offended by all the sins of mankind.

Why is this the case? As we have seen, Aquinas states that Christ's suffering has value because of his charity and obedience, and because of his suffering, which is a tangible sign of this charity and obedience. In a manner which remains veiled in mystery, Christ's sufferings show the depths to which sin offends God, while at the same time they offer atonement for sin.

The pain which Christ endures makes up for the excessive self-love at the root of sin. As Aquinas points out, it is appropriate that the disorder of sin be met with punishment, so as to restore the order of justice. The act of suffering helps to correct this disorder: "It is just that he who has been too indulgent to his will, should suffer something against his will, for thus will equality be restored."

But beyond the reality of sin and the need for atonement, Christ's sufferings reveal in a new way the immense depths of God's love for the human race. Jutta Burggraf points out that we might understand Christ's passion as a manifestation that Christ "is capable of doing and giving *everything* for us, like a friend who dies to save another." In choosing this particular manner of saving us, she notes, God shows in a definitive way his love for each and every human being.

Christ's charity, present in his human will, reconstitutes that order which had been lost in Adam's sin. This order, as the American Dominican theologian Romanus Cessario comments, entails "a complete submission and subjection of all human energies and interests to God." Such an order of justice is not an abstract concept, but a justice which is united to God's charity, and made concretely present in the person of Christ. Through Christ's sharing in our human nature, his justice implies a restoration of our communion with the Trinity.

Christ's passion is not simply "enough" to make up for the sins of man; it is *superabundant* or "more than enough." As St. John Paul II affirmed, Christ's suffering and death manifest a "superabundance of love" which overcomes every human sin. Because of Christ's identity, any act of charity and obedience on his part would be enough to make satisfaction for sin. In making superabundant satisfaction, God shows the depths of his love and the fullness of his victory over sin. Michael Schmaus observed that "in Jesus a power of love and truth was operative which surpassed all the forces of evil and falsehood" (see 1 Pt 1:18–23; Rom 5:20).

Mankind is indeed deserving of punishment for sin, but we should not consider Christ's passion and death to be a punishment in the strict sense. This erroneous position, known as *penal substitution,* would mean that Christ was punished for our sins as if he himself had committed them. The Protestant Reformers Martin Luther and John Calvin held to this view. This position would imply that Christ himself was somehow held as being "guilty" of sin and Christ would be subject to the Father's anger at sin.

Penal substitution is wrong because Christ remained always sinless and always beloved by the Father. Still, we can say that Christ himself has made expiation for *our* sins by his suffering. He has compensated for the duty of punishment which was due to us for our sins.

The suffering of Christ has its value not because it is a punishment, but precisely due to *love.* In sin, we turn our will away from God, and it is only in charity that the proper order of the will is restored. Love is the difference between simply accepting a punishment and genuine *satisfaction.* Without charity, as Aquinas affirms, works of satisfaction are not acceptable to God.

We might think of the example of a child who disobeys his parents. The parents might impose a punishment, such as not being able to play with toys. The parents take away the toys so that the child is forced to observe the punishment. Still, so long as the child is angry and upset about this, the relationship between child and parents has not been restored. Only if the child accepts the punishment willingly, out of concern for his parents, has the relationship been repaired. In this case, the child's satisfaction for his fault is moved by charity.

With regard to the Redemption achieved by Christ, satisfaction is achieved in a way which fully atones for our sins but also involves our *freedom*. Christ's offering of himself on the Cross is a free act by which he accepts the will of the Father. As in all of the other mysteries of his life, on the Cross Christ offers us the grace of salvation and he also *shows* us the path to true satisfaction. We must freely open our heart to receive the gift of salvation. We are called to be identified with the sentiments of Christ on the Cross and to share in Christ's desires to make satisfaction for all sins.

In summary, then, satisfaction means that Christ fully makes atonement for the offense caused by the sins of mankind. Christ does this by freely taking on our human nature, so that his merits are united to those of the human race. In his entire life, Jesus accepts the limits of the human condition, including the reality of suffering. He does this in a singular way in his suffering and death. Through the offering of himself on the Cross in charity and obedience, Christ makes an oblation which more than offsets the evil of mankind.

In choosing this particular path of making satisfaction, Christ reveals the sad reality of sin as an offense against God, but most importantly he reveals the depth of God's love for us. Today, there is a strong tendency, within theology and in the Church, to emphasize that the Cross is a sign of God's love. This is certainly very important, but this truth should not lead us to forget the reality that God's love is also connected with his justice. Christ makes satisfaction in such a way that he reminds us that sin truly is an offense against God and leads to a real disorder in the person and in creation.

God, in his perfect justice, does not simply ignore sin. The Father's will is that out of God's abundant love, Christ—as the Council of Trent affirmed—"merited Justification for us by His most holy Passion on the wood of the cross, and made satisfaction for us unto God the Father." By this satisfaction, the Holy Trinity heals and renews the wounds caused by our sad choice of evil.

CHAPTER 8

The Redemptive Value of the Sacrifice of Christ (II)

Blessed may you be, my Lord Jesus Christ. You redeemed our souls with your precious blood and most holy death, and in your mercy you led them from exile back to eternal life.

—St. Bridget of Sweden

The categories of merit and satisfaction, as we have seen in the last chapter, offer us important insights into the meaning of Christ's redemption. These notions remind us that Christ has won for us the grace of salvation which we could not obtain on our own. However, these categories offer only partial insights into the rich meaning of Christ's redemptive act at Calvary. To give a more complete picture, this chapter will examine in more detail two important scriptural concepts for understanding Christ's death on the Cross. These notions are *sacrifice* and *redemption*.

A. Sacrifice in the Old Testament

The word *sacrifice* has a fairly negative connotation among many people today. The term conveys the sense that we are giving up something good, and therefore it is something that we don't look forward to. However, the original sense of sacrifice is something positive. It comes from the Latin *sacrificium*, which literally means "making sacred." The word conveys the sense that there is a transfer of ownership, usually to God. A sacrifice is therefore defined not so much as what is given up, but *to whom* the sacrifice is offered.

Throughout history, inside and outside of the Bible, people have felt the need to offer sacrifice to God. By means of sacrifice, human beings recognize God's dominion and manifest their own need to acknowledge this authority.

Sacrifices can be a profession of God's identity as Lord, but they also reveal our identity. Sacrifices remind us that we are called to respond to God not simply with words and good intentions but with our whole person. In carrying out sacrifice, we show our need to offer up something material as a sign of our submission to God. The most important sacrifices in the ancient world involved animals, which in the pagan world were associated with the gods.

The Chosen People took up the human reality of sacrifice and raised this practice to its authentic meaning: an act of adoration of the one God. These sacrifices in Israel are distinct from pagan sacrifices, in that they reflect the personal relationship which God establishes with his people. Pagan sacrifices, on the other hand, could be directed to any number of gods or even to illustrious persons.

In the case of the People of Israel, sacrifices had both a profound spiritual orientation and an essential physical aspect. After the covenant given through Moses at Mount Sinai, the sacrifices were offered within the concrete places associated with the presence of God: at first in the tabernacle, or tent sanctuary which the Chosen People transported through the wilderness, and later in the temple.

The excellence of these sacrifices is seen in the first of the sacrifices mentioned in the Book of Leviticus: the *holocaust*. The word literally means "burnt in its entirety." In this sacrifice, the victim was incinerated as a recognition of God's absolute dominion. This type of sacrifice was not common among neighboring peoples, but in Israel the practice had a prime importance from very early on. The details involved in the holocaust reveal the extent to which these sacrifices reflected a true act of adoration. The Chosen People recognized that the burning of the offering on the altar was particularly acceptable to God, creating "a pleasing odor to the Lord" (Lv 1:13). God calls his people to offer a victim "without blemish" (Lv 1:3), the best they can offer. The person making the offering would lay his hands on the victim, and thus identify himself with what was being presented. Priests would carry out the actual sacrifice.

Blood was an important aspect of the holocaust. In Israel, blood was seen as the source of life, and for this reason it was associated with God. In contrast to the sacrifices of other religions, the shedding of blood took on a central role in the Old Testament. Blood was given by God to his people in worship, so that they might receive the forgiveness of sins: "for it is the blood that makes atonement, by reason of the life" (Lv 17:11).

In addition to the holocaust, the Old Testament relates a set of other sacrifices which expressed different aspects of the Chosen People's relationship with God. These offerings included *oblations* of agricultural produce, which is a very ancient type of sacrifice. The external characteristics of this type of sacrifice reveal the attitude of adoration which God asks for. Among the ancient peoples in the biblical world, it was common to offer God the first yield of each year's crop. The Book of Leviticus emphasizes that a baked grain offering should be made with the finest of flour, that of wheat, and be accompanied by frankincense, a powder composed of fine spices. Leaven and honey were excluded from the offerings because they were seen as agents of corruption; salt on the other hand was added because it preserved the quality of the food (Lv 2:11–13).

While holocausts and oblations show the totality of the offering made to God, the *peace offering* or *communion offering* was a sign of communion between humanity and God. These offerings were animal sacrifices which involved blood. They express communion in the fact that not all of the victim was burnt. It was only partially destroyed, and the rest was eaten by the priests or the persons making the sacrifice (see Dt 12:27). In this way, God and man "shared" the offering.

Sin offerings are of particular importance for understanding Christ's sacrifice. They were offered in ancient times by other peoples in Canaan. These sacrifices take on a particular importance in light of the special covenant between God and his people. Sin was understood as a violation of the relationship of the Chosen People with God, either voluntary or involuntary.

These sins were not necessarily sins as we understand them, in the sense of a violation of the moral law. These so-called sins could involve simply the transgression of the specific rules which God had given to his people. Still, these actions broke with God's prescriptions and therefore needed to be treated with seriousness. Any such act, as the Franciscan scripture scholar Roland J. Faley noted, "disturbed the right order of things," and it was necessary to offer a sacrifice as atonement.

The Book of Leviticus first speaks of sin offerings as being made for the sins of the priest (Lv 4:3). This reference shows the awareness of the particular seriousness of sins committed by the priest, which bring guilt upon the whole people. Sin offerings were also presented to God for the whole people of Israel: its rulers, individuals, poor persons who could not afford the animal offering, and other specific sins (Lv 4–5).

The sins of the priest and the whole people of Israel required that the animal sacrifice be burnt outside the camp, that is, outside the camp in the wilderness which the people inhabited (Lv 4:12, 21). Going "outside the camp" meant leaving the holy camp of the Chosen People, and was a sign of the uncleanness incurred by sin. The burning of the entire animal was an expression of sorrow for having sinned, since the person making the offering could not eat the meat of the victim.

Sin offerings involved an animal victim, but the key element for expiating sins was the sprinkling of blood. This act took place at either the altar outside the tabernacle or upon the veil which separated the people from the Holy of Holies, the inner holy space where the ark of the covenant was kept.

B. The Sacrifices of the Old Testament Fulfilled in Christ

Sacrifices were a primary means by which the People of Israel worshipped God. Among the other motives for these rituals, the people were deeply aware of their sinfulness, and sacrifices were an essential way by which they sought purification. These offerings were not only an expression of God's mercy but also of the reality of human freedom, since they required the people's free response to God.

Still, the Old Testament recognizes the limits of sacrifice. Some Scripture scholars are of the opinion that the sacrifices of the Old Testament were not meant to atone for sin, understood as a deliberate offense against God. According to this view, the sacrifices for sin would atone instead for ignorance or mistakes (see Lv 4:2; Heb 5:2). A deliberate turning away from God, on the other hand, would mean that the person must be "be cut off from among his people" (Lv 17:4), so that the whole community would not be contaminated by the sin.

The precise aim of sin offerings is not clear, which is not surprising since the nature of sin is not as clear in the Old Testament as in the New. Whatever the case might be, the Old Testament offers less security that sin in the deepest sense can be forgiven. All the same, the Chosen People desire such forgiveness. As the psalmist prays, after recognizing his guilt: "Wash me thoroughly from my iniquity, and cleanse me from my sin!" (Ps 51:2).

In spite of these sincere desires for pardon, Thomas Aquinas observes that if the Old Testament sacrifices are able to take away sins, "it was due to the power of Christ's blood." The sacrifices of the Old Law only prefigure the perfect sin offering which would be accomplished by Christ.

The prophets would often draw attention to the inadequacy so often present in the sacrifices of the Old Law. They did not condemn sacrifices as such, but the improper dispositions with which they were carried out. Such bad dispositions included an excessive focus on ritual, which led persons to lose sight of the meaning of ritual; they also included magical ideas of sacrifice. With such dispositions, the rituals of sacrifice can actually become an offense to God:

> What to me is the multitude of your sacrifices? says the
> LORD; I have had enough of burnt offerings of rams and the
> fat of fed beasts; I do not delight in the blood of bulls, or of
> lambs, or of he-goats. (Is 1:11)

Through these critiques, the prophets brought about a *spiritualization* of the notion of sacrifice. They recognized that the outward observances connected with these rituals were meant to be the reflection of a deeper interior attitude of holiness present in man's heart. However, this realization itself reveals the inadequacy of the sacrifices of the Old Law and looks forward to the future. As Christology specialist Antonio Ducay notes, the prophets realize that "salvation will have to arise from a new and definitive divine gift, capable of changing the heart, transforming hardness of heart into prompt docility."

As we know, God offered this divine gift by means of the life, death, and resurrection of Jesus Christ and the sending of the Holy Spirit. Through this divine action, Christ offers the definitive and perfect sacrifice, and he enables us to offer a sacrifice which might be truly pleasing to God.

Jesus did not deny the importance of the sacrifices commanded in the Old Law. Like the prophets, he speaks of the need for sacrifices to be accompanied by a true desire for adoration and by purity of heart (see Mt 9:13, 12:7). At the same time, Jesus makes it clear that these old sacrifices are secondary and will give way to a new order of worship. As he affirms in reference to his own mission, "something greater than the temple is here" (Mt 12:6). This new cult is focused not on any physical place, however holy it might be. Jesus tells the Samaritan woman that the time of worship that is focused on a particular locale, whether mountain or temple, is coming to an end. Rather, "the hour is coming, and now is, when the true worshipers will worship the Father in spirit and truth" (Jn 4:23).

This new pattern of worship is above all Christ himself, through whom we can enter into the intimacy of God's own life. Jesus himself brings to fulfillment the qualities desired by God in the old sacrifices. He is the true victim, perfect and without blemish, who can really stand in our place to make atonement. He offers himself completely, in his life and in his death on the Cross, and in doing so he shows the full meaning of holocaust as adoration. By his partaking of the human and divine natures, he is able to bring about the communion between God and man desired through the peace offerings. Christ's blood shed on the Cross accomplishes the expiation which was symbolized, though not truly realized, by the blood shed in the old sacrifices.

More specifically, Christ's passion and death bring to fulfillment three particular sacrifices of the Old Law. In the first place, in the institution of the Eucharist, Christ identifies his own sacrifice on the Cross with the *blood of the covenant*: "[H]e took a cup, and when he had given thanks he gave it to them, saying, 'Drink of it, all of you; for this is my blood of the covenant, which is

poured out for many for the forgiveness of sins' "(Mt 26:27–28).
These words recall the blood which is the sign of the covenant
enacted on Mount Sinai (Ex 24:6–8). This blood served as a sign
of the solemn covenant which God entered into with Israel.

In this important Old Testament episode, the sacrifice is
offered by Moses and a group of young men, since the priesthood
of the Old Covenant has not yet been established. The group of
young men offer a sacrifice to God from the slope of Mount Sinai.
Moses takes the blood and sprinkles half of it on the altar and half
of it upon the people. In this way, the blood forms a bond of communion between God and his people. Given the sacredness of
blood, the sprinkling shows God's presence among his people but
also that the Chosen People are now a people specially dedicated
to God, "a kingdom of priests and a holy nation" (Ex 19:6). We
should also note that this covenant is part of a meal (Ex 24:11),
which was a common way of sealing a pact at the time.

In Christ's words and deeds at the Last Supper, these rites
of the Old Testament achieve their full meaning. Christ's blood,
offered on the Cross and made present in the sacrament of the
Eucharist, seals the new covenant that God makes with his people through the only-begotten Son. Christ's blood is the sign and
life-giving source which ratifies this new covenant. Through this
blood Jesus brings about a new People of God, which as the Second Vatican Council's Constitution *Lumen Gentium* affirmed,
is "made up of Jew and gentile, making them one, not according
to the flesh but in the Spirit." Christ institutes the ministerial
priesthood, and by his blood he constitutes, in a certain way, all
of his people as "priests to his God and Father" (Rv 1:6).

The second of the key sacrifices fulfilled in Christ is the *Passover sacrifice*. The word *passover* echoes the Hebrew verb *pasha,*
which means "pass over." The term indicates that the Passover
commemoration was instituted to recall the deliverance of Israel
from Egypt. In this important moment of liberation, God smites

the firstborn males in Egypt but "passes over" the firstborn of the Israelites (Ex 12:12).

The animal victim in the Passover sacrifice, as in the original liberation of the Chosen People, is the lamb (Ex 12:5). As in the case of the sacrifices later prescribed by God, the key element in expiation is again the blood. God proclaims to his people, while still in Egypt, that "[t]he blood shall be a sign for you . . . when I see the blood, I will pass over you, and no plague shall fall upon you to destroy you, when I smite the land of Egypt" (Ex 12:13). In this case the blood was not directly connected with the remission of sins but with God's power against the presence of evil.

The sacrifice of the lamb had a significance which went beyond the specific Passover rite. The Chosen People were commanded to offer two lambs each day upon the altar, which served as a continual reminder of their liberation from Egypt (Ex 29:38, 29:46). This sacrifice was the most important of all the sacrifices offered by the people.

Already in the Old Testament, in the Book of Isaiah, the Suffering Servant is portrayed as a lamb which is offered in expiation. The lamb is a young sheep, and sheep themselves were associated with meekness and innocence. The comparison with the lamb expresses the servant's ready obedience, even in being led to slaughter (Is 53:7). The image of the lamb, in relation to Christ, therefore, indicates his redemptive identity. At the same time, this figure also emphasizes Christ's humanity, since the Bible uses the lamb as a metaphor for the Chosen People in their relationship with God, who is seen as shepherd (Ps 23).

The Passover was a defining moment in the life of the Old Testament People of God, and the New Testament uses Passover imagery as a way of understanding Christ's sacrifice. In keeping with the importance of the lamb sacrifices, St. John fittingly describes Jesus as "the Lamb of God" in his Gospel (1:29, 1:36). In the First Letter of St. Peter, Christ is compared to "a lamb without blemish or spot" (1:19). More broadly, the New Testament authors recognized that Christ's sacrifice was a defining moment of liberation, like the Passover. They realized that Christ's sacrifice rescues us from the true evil, sin, and that this sacrifice fulfilled and surpassed the old Passover.

The Last Supper, as we have noted, takes place in a Passover setting even though it was distinct from the Passover rite. St. John's account of the Crucifixion recounts that Christ is sacrificed on the Cross at the very moment in which the paschal lambs were slaughtered in the Jewish Passover. According to the Passover rite, no bone of the lamb was to be broken (Ex 12:46). As Joseph Ratzinger comments, "Jesus appears here as the true Paschal Lamb, pure and whole."

The early Christians' awareness of Christ as Lamb of God led them to be more keenly conscious of the definitive liberation they had received through Christ's death and resurrection. These climactic events of Christ's life would come to be known precisely as the *paschal* mystery. St. Paul exhorts the Corinthians to put away malice and walk in truth, with the knowledge that "Christ, our paschal lamb, has been sacrificed" (1 Cor 5:7).

The third key Old Testament sacrifice fully realized in Christ was the sacrifice of the *Day of Atonement* (Lv 16). We have mentioned this commemoration in chapter two with regard to the priestly mediation of Christ. This moment was the most solemn day of the Jewish calendar, and despite its penitential character it was also one of the most joyful days. The high priest would offer the sacrifice of a bull for sins of the priests and a goat for the sins of the people. Once more, the key moment of expiation was the sprinkling of blood. It was only on this day that the high priest would pass through the veil in the tabernacle and enter into the innermost space, the Holy of Holies.

The priest would then incense the propitiatory or *mercy seat*, which was the special place of contact between God and his people (Ex 25:22). This "seat" was the gold lid which covered the ark of the covenant, the container which held the stone tablets with the Ten Commandments inscribed upon them. The priest would sprinkle the blood of the sacrifices upon the mercy seat. He would then invoke the holy name of Yahweh, the only time this was done all year. These actions sought to bring about expiation for the sins of the priests and people. In addition, the priest would lay his hands on the remaining goat (the other goat was sacrificed to God), and confess the sins of the people. In this way, the sins were "transmitted" to the goat, which was then led off into the desert, thought to be the place of evil spirits.

This sacrifice of the Day of Atonement has the same common denominator as the sacrifice of the covenant. The sacrifice of the covenant was a solemn beginning to God's union with his people, and the sacrifice of atonement was meant to re-establish this union. In both sacrifices, blood is the special sign of God's bond with Israel. It is a sign not simply of the remission of sins, but above all it is a positive symbol of God's relationship of love with his people. The author of the Letter to the Hebrews sees the solemn sacrifice of atonement as a forerunner of the singularity of Christ's sacrifice (9:6–12). Still, in contrast to Christ's sacrifice, the sacrifice of atonement needed to be repeated yearly.

Christ, on the other hand, "high priest of the good things that have come . . . entered once for all into the Holy Place, taking not the blood of goats and calves but his own blood, thus securing an eternal redemption" (Heb 9:11–12). This "Holy Place" is no longer a physical place but heaven itself, the place of definitive communion with God (see Heb 9:24). This perfect sacrifice is offered by the holy humanity of Christ in the power of the Holy Spirit (see Heb 9:14).

This sacrifice brings to fulfillment *all* of the sacrifices of the Old Testament. As St. Paul affirms, Christ is the one whom the Father "put forward as an expiation by his blood, to be received by faith," thus showing God's "righteousness" and "forbearance" (Rom 3:25). This is the sacrifice which brings about the genuine satisfaction for sins and communion with God which the old sacrifices sought but could not truly bring about.

As we have seen in the last chapter, the redeeming value of Christ's sacrifice occurs through his *charity*. Christ's blood, shed on the Cross, is the great sign of his love. While remaining innocent and sinless, Christ's charity in a mysterious way takes on our sins and brings about the destruction of sin.

The author of the Letter to the Hebrews points out that Jesus suffered "outside the gate," like the sacrifices for sin which were offered outside the camp (13:11–12). This exclusion shows the extent to which Christ, in his charity, has taken on the reality of sin "in order to sanctify the people through his own blood" (Hebrews 13:12). This charity, which is accompanied by Christ's perfect *justice*, makes sufficient and in fact *superabundant* reparation for sins.

Throughout the centuries, the Church's Tradition has continued to reflect on the rich meaning of Christ's death as sacrifice, emphasizing different aspects of this deep mystery. The Greek Fathers of the Church echoed the scriptural texts about Christ's sacrifice as expiation for sins. They emphasized the "divinization" which has occurred as a fruit of Christ's redeeming act. Because Christ has real human flesh, and at the same time a divine nature, his sacrifice can bring divine life to man. Through this divinization, God has re-created human nature and raised it to the supernatural level. The Latin Fathers, complementing this view, see Christ as the mediator who can truly repair the wound to human nature and offense to God's justice caused by sin.

In Christ's perfect sacrifice, Jesus serves as *victim*, and at the same time he himself is the *priest*. He is both a victim who passively accepts his condemnation and suffering, and at the same time the priest who voluntarily makes an offering of himself.

As the twentieth-century German Scripture scholar Johannes Behm observes, this sacrifice is "a free, personal act of self-giving which the sinless and eternal Son accomplishes once for all." In this act, the holiness of mankind reaches its highest point. This one sacrifice, which remains present in the Sacrifice of the Mass, is the model of sanctity for the Christian. All of the faithful, in living union with Jesus' sacrifice and in imitation of it, are called to offer themselves as "a living sacrifice, holy and acceptable to God" (Rom 12:1).

C. Christ's Death as Ransom and Redemption

The analysis of satisfaction undertaken in the last chapter helps us to understand the biblical language of *ransom* and *redemption*. These notions, as we have seen in chapter two, are closely related in the Greek language and they indicated the payment of a debt. The *ransom* is the sum one would need to pay to liberate a slave or a prisoner; *redemption* is the act by which the ransom is paid and the person is set free. The words are somewhat interchangeable, and we can also say that a person has been "ransomed" when he has been redeemed.

Still, as we have also seen in chapter two, the Hebrew word *gaal* has a broader sense than simply an economic or legal liberation. In addition to the sense of payment, *gaal* conveys the sense of family belonging. This family tie leads a family member to protect the other family member who is in a dire state, and therefore to pay the necessary ransom price.

The concepts of ransom and redemption were used in the Old Testament to describe the more profound debt which man owes to God. However, in the Old Testament redemption is not simply an act of liberation from a precarious state. Redemption has an eminently positive meaning: it refers to how God has "acquired for himself" or taken possession of his people.

In light of the linguistic background, we can appreciate how the words *ransom* and *redemption* have a range of meanings, which help to convey the profound mystery of salvation. When the Old Testament was translated into Greek, the Greek word for ransom came to take on some of the different senses of the Hebrew notions of ransom and redemption. One meaning of ransom is a gift which takes the place of a fault. This gift might at times be money, but above all it indicates a certain equality. This equality implies giving a gift which is the equivalent of what was taken, in keeping with the ancient logic of "you shall give life for life, eye for eye, tooth for tooth" (Ex 21:23–24). The word ransom could also be used in Greek for the Hebrew *gaal*, which had the more specific sense of redeeming a family member from bondage.

These connotations regarding ransom and redemption have an important role in the New Testament. Christ himself seems to accept the logic of "life for life" when he announces that he will offer himself in ransom: "[T]he Son of man also came not to be served but to serve, and to give his life as a ransom for many" (Mk 10:45). Christ indicates here that the sacrifice of his life is an offering of sufficient value to bring about the freedom of man, who exists in a stage of bondage due to sin and its consequences.

The language of ransom fittingly expresses the profound liberation that Christ has won. This terminology also reminds us of the extent to which Christ has fulfilled God's justice so as to bring about this emancipation. St. Peter reminds Christians that they "were ransomed from the futile ways inherited from your fathers, not with perishable things such as silver or gold, but with the precious blood of Christ." (1 Pt 1:18–19). For St. Paul, the awareness of this "price" paid by God is a reminder of the need to live in profound adoration of God: "You are not your own; you were bought with a price. So glorify God in your body" (1 Cor 6:19–20).

While the notions of ransom and redemption express the deep reality of sin and the need for satisfaction, this language has its limits. Christ offers up superabundant atonement for the sins of men, but nowhere does Scripture imply that this price is demanded of God. God is not obligated to pay the debt incurred by man's sin. The offering of the Son of God is not the implementation of a "contract," required by justice, but rather is better described as an *exchange*.

The Old Testament recognizes that God is not bound by the system of ransom. God does not need to pay a ransom, because he has dominion over all things. In promising liberation to the Chosen People, God tells them "you shall be redeemed without money" (Is 52:3). In this freedom from the obligation to ransom, we can see that the Redemption, while an act of infinite justice, is at the same an utterly gratuitous act of God's love. To use words from Christ at his own baptism, God sees it as "fitting" to perform all justice through the salvific mission and sacrifice of Christ (Mt 3:15), even though God was not obligated to act in this way.

Within the Old Testament perspective, while maintaining the connection with expiation for sin, *redemption* comes to have a broader meaning than simply *ransom*. Redemption has an original association with the sense of payment, but more profoundly it is, as the German Old Testament scholar Otto Proksch states, "a free act of God's grace which embraces the Gentiles too." Redemption is a gift of God's love which man does not and cannot merit.

Moreover, redemption has an essential *filial* aspect in the New Testament, in keeping with the original sense of the Hebrew *gaal*. It is not simply an economic or legal transaction which allows for freedom, but a means by which God the Father recognizes and fulfills the "family tie," specifically the paternity, which he has toward us. As St. Paul affirms, "when the time had fully come, God sent forth his Son, born of woman, born under the law, to redeem those who were under the law, so that we might receive adoption as sons" (Gal 4:4–5). This liberation involves our elevation to the level of being sons and daughters of God, a state which far surpasses the human sense of being redeemed from human servitude or debt.

In examining the concepts of redemption and ransom, we should always keep in mind that these words are not simply literary figures for God's love. Christ's redemption can never be reduced to simply a symbol, as many have done in recent years. Christ's sacrifice is *efficacious*: It brings about the union with God and atonement for sins which we seek, but cannot attain, in the other sacrifices. Christ's offering of himself, in particular his passion and death, truly liberate us from a real state of slavery.

Christ's saving work has brought about a destruction of the power of sin and given to us freedom from the punishment due to sin. Jesus' perfect sacrifice has undone the curse pronounced after man's first sin. Christ has won a *triple victory* over those enemies which defeated Adam and Eve, and which have continued to strongly influence the human race throughout history: sin, the power of the devil, and death. By this triumph, the human race has been enabled to walk in "newness of life" (Rom 6:4), in friendship with God and according to the model of Christ. The meaning of this victory of Christ, as it unfolds in the life of the Christian, will be discussed in more detail in chapter ten.

A final important characteristic of the Redemption is its *universality*. Universality includes the truth that, as we have noted in chapter two, Christ is the *only* Savior of mankind. Only his sacrifice and his mediation can lead man to God. Universality also implies that Christ has died for *all* of the human race, whether past, present, or future.

As we have also seen, St. Paul recognizes that just as Adam's fault has led to a state of sinfulness for all humanity, Christ's death and resurrection have brought about the gift of salvation for the entire human race (Rom 5:15–18). The Church has had to repeat this truth in the face of some who say that persons are predestined to damnation. Such notions were present in the teaching of the German monk and theologian Gottschalk of Orbais in the ninth century. Later the same ideas would be associated with the French Protestant reformer John Calvin in the sixteenth century, as well as the Dutch Catholic theologian and bishop Cornelius Jansen in the seventeenth century.

Certainly, the universal scope of Christ's death is not easy to understand. The Church reminds us of the sad reality of hell, for those who freely reject the gift of redemption. Christ has won the grace of redemption for all, but each person must freely accept this gift. Jesus has opened the path to eternal life and shows us the way to overcome sin, but we in our freedom must choose to make this gift our own.

We should not see God's respect for freedom as a limitation on the efficacy of the Redemption accomplished in Christ. Rather, just as Christ had a real human freedom and uses this freedom in the fullest way, our liberty before the Redemption shows the greatness of God's gift. God has redeemed us, but he has not "taken over" our wills. He has allowed the possibility that we ourselves, with the free gift from on high, might realize our own freedom in the most profound way. A redemption which did not respect and give meaning to this great gift, freedom, would not really be our Redemption.

The redemption of man, then, shows forth both the grandeur of God and the true splendor of the human person. It is not simply the work of Christ which brings about our salvation; it is also our personal *confession* of faith in him, moved by grace, which makes salvation an effective reality. This confession is in the first place the result of the action of the Holy Spirit, but also requires a genuine human cooperation. God desires that each of us, freely, accept and assimilate the mystery of the Incarnation and Redemption into our own life. If we open our heart to God in this way, this incorporation into Christ, in the words of St. John Paul II, "bears fruit not only of adoration of God but also of deep wonder at himself."

Finally, the universality of redemption further means that God makes this gift available to all. The Second Vatican Council affirmed the New Testament truth that God wants all to be saved (1 Tm 2:4) and also taught that God gives each person the possibility of receiving salvation. The Council's Constitution *Lumen Gentium* states that even those who, through no fault of their own, "have not yet arrived at an explicit knowledge of God" can receive the fruits of Christ's saving work.

Even in such cases, there remains the necessity for the grace won by Christ. This grace is offered to us through the mediation of the Church, even when we are not conscious of it. In these more extraordinary actions of grace, there is also a need for us to exercise freedom so as to accept the invitation to receive redemption. God makes this invitation present in the depth of our conscience.

How this universal redemption works in the soul of each person is a great mystery. Still, the possibility for all to receive salvation shows forth in a splendid way the full power of the Redemption. Even in the many difficult situations marked by sin, suffering, and death, Christians are called to live with the firm conviction that God's superabundant redemption is at work.

CHAPTER 9

———

Christ's Glorification:
The Resurrection and Ascension

Christ, through his Resurrection, has so to speak "justified" the work of creation, and especially the creation of man. He has "justified" it in the sense that he has revealed the "just measure" of good intended by God at the beginning of human history.

—*St. John Paul II*, Memory and Identity

A. The Burial and Descent of Christ to Hell

The burial of Christ in a tomb manifests the reality of Christ's death. This tomb would also become the great sign of the Resurrection. Just as in the case of any human death, the soul of Jesus was separated from his body. Christ's dead body was indeed a lifeless body.

Still, this corpse was not the same as any dead body. Through the hypostatic union, by which the divine and human natures are united in the one person of Christ, Christ's dead body remained united to the divine Person of the Son. Because of this divine power, Thomas Aquinas holds that Christ's corpse did not undergo decay, in fulfillment of the words of the psalm: "Nor wilt Thou suffer Thy holy one to see corruption" (Ps 16:10, Aquinas' translation).

Jesus' burial offers a point of connection between his death and resurrection. The Evangelists recount that Christ needed to be buried with haste. According to Jewish law, bodies had to be

buried before the coming of the Sabbath, when such work was
not permitted. Just as in the case of the Passover lambs that were
being sacrificed at the time of Christ's death—as we have noted
in chapter eight—no bones of Christ were broken. Instead, a sol-
dier pierced Jesus' right side, where the heart is located, "and at
once there came out blood and water" (Jn 19:34).

It seems that St. John himself, along with the later tradition of the Church, sees the blood and water as symbols for
the sacraments and in particular for baptism and the Eucharist.
These signs show that, with Christ's very death, the fruits of the
Redemption have been obtained.

The holiness of Christ's dead body is also seen in the way
the corpse is treated. Despite Christ's life of poverty and igno-
minious death, he is placed in a tomb which is dug within rock.
Such a burial site was the privilege of wealthy Jews. Two afflu-
ent members of the Sanhedrin, Joseph of Arimathea and Nico-
demus, embalm Jesus' body with a hundred pounds' weight of a
mixture of myrrh and aloes. This quantity is out of the ordinary
and would be fitting for a royal burial. Joseph Ratzinger comments: "Just when it seems that everything is finished, his glory
mysteriously shines through." In these and the other extraordinary signs which accompany Christ's death (see Mt 27:51–54),
we see that Christ's death already contains the beginning of his
glorious resurrection.

Christ's death is also the beginning of the moment in which
humanity begins to receive the saving fruits of Christ's death.
St. Peter notes that while Jesus' body is dead, his spirit remains
alive and "he went and preached to the spirits in prison" (1 Pt
3:19). The Church has understood this text as referring to the
truth that Christ "descended into hell," as mentioned in the
Apostles' Creed.

This "hell" is not the hell which is the place of eternal punishment. Rather, this hell has the more general sense implied by

the Hebrew word *sheol*, which means "place of the dead" (see Acts 2:31). Christ descended into this place of the dead, so as to free the just who lived before him. This descent shows that even the just could only enter into heaven as fruit of the Savior's sacrifice on behalf of all humanity.

In Christ's burial and descent to the realm of the dead, we can appreciate the extent to which Jesus has identified himself with the human condition, while at the same time remaining true God. He fully takes on the reality of death, and even draws close to the just who have died and are not yet able to attain salvation. The descent to hell shows Christ's desire to bring salvation to all those who await him, both before Christ but also after the Son of God's coming to earth. The Church trusts that all persons, including those who have not explicitly come to faith in Christ and yet have sought to live a just life, can receive the fruits of Christ's total offering of himself.

B. The Event of the Resurrection

Holy Saturday, the day in which the corpse of Christ lies in the tomb, "reveals God's great sabbath rest" (*Catechism of the Catholic Church*, 624). The body of Christ, though lifeless, follows the pattern of Sabbath rest. On the following dawn, the first day of the week, God inaugurates a new era of salvation. Christ's obedience brings about the decisive victory over sin and death. This is a triumph which obedience to the Old Law could never accomplish.

Christ's resurrection fulfills the notions of resurrection found in the Old Testament. The idea of resurrection itself was a distinctive belief of the Chosen People. Most ancient religions had an awareness of life *after* death, but such an afterlife is different from *resurrection*. In the ancient view, the soul was seen as immortal, but it would become separated from the body at death. Resurrection, on the other hand, implies that death has been reversed. The soul and body become united once again and life is restored.

Even though the pagan mind had the awareness of life after death, the idea of an authentic resurrection was a true novelty. The Greeks at the Areopagus are taken by surprise when St. Paul brings up the doctrine of the resurrection of the dead (see Acts 17:32). Nonetheless, Israel's special awareness of God's power led it to conceive of resurrection as a special manifestation of God's power. The Old Testament reveals that God is Lord of life and death: "The LORD kills and brings to life; he brings down to Sheol and raises up" (1 Sm 2:6).

The resurrection miracles carried out by Elijah and Elisha show that the language of resurrection is not simply metaphorical (1 Kgs 17:17–32; 2 Kgs 4:32–35). God reveals his divine power precisely in being able to reverse the normal course of death and restore life. Through the painful experience of the exile, God led the Chosen People to a clearer belief in a concrete bodily resurrection (see Dn 12:2–3; 2 Mc 7:9).

References to resurrection in the Old Testament at times refer to the resurrection of individual bodies. At other times, the reference to resurrection is less direct and can be understood in a metaphorical way. God promises his people, suffering from the exile, that he will grant them new life: "Thus says the Lord GOD to these bones: Behold, I will cause breath to enter you, and you shall live" (Ez 37:5) This restoration makes most immediate reference to God's work of revitalizing his people and bringing them back to their homeland. Still, at the same time, this renewal points toward the definitive restoration which will occur in the resurrection of the dead: "And I will lay sinews upon you, and will cause flesh to come upon you, and cover you with skin, and put breath in you, and you shall live; and you shall know that I am the LORD" (Ez 37:6).

The Old Testament shows the development of a belief in resurrection which becomes clearer in the centuries previous to Christ. However, it is important to note that the resurrection of the dead was not a frequent topic in the Old Testament, and was not thought to be an event which would occur in the present age. The resurrection was seen as far off. It was an event which would mark the end of the current age and the beginning of a new age in which Israel would be restored. The hope for the future resurrection was not connected to the expectation of a future messiah.

In this context of Jewish expectation, the transformative event which occurred on the first Easter morning came as a great surprise. Even so, Christ's rising from the tomb was also a fulfillment of the Jewish expectations of the resurrection.

The resurrection becomes much more of a central theme in the New Testament than in the Old. St. Paul passes on to the Corinthians the message of "first importance" that Christ died for our sins, was buried, as "was raised on the third day in accordance with the scriptures" (1 Cor 15:4). Christ's resurrection is the key evidence for the truth of Christ's mission, and the primary model for the new life which Christians are called to lead.

The Gospel accounts convey the sense of surprise and bewilderment at the first announcement of Christ's triumph over death. This shock reminds us that the first disciples found themselves in the presence of a real event which was unprecedented in human history. With time, they would come to see that this occurrence was the fulfillment of what God's plan had foretold in the Scriptures.

St. Mark's account of the Resurrection, in chapter sixteen of his Gospel, particularly captures the element of surprise. Mary Magdalene and some other women go to anoint the body of Jesus the morning after the Sabbath, and they encounter the initial sign of the Resurrection: the *empty tomb* (Mk 16:6). The vacant sepulcher shows the actualization of the prophecy of the Old Testament, cited by St. Peter at Pentecost, that the soul of God's "Holy One" would not see corruption or be abandoned to the place of the dead (Acts 2:27).

In the face of the radical newness of Christ's rising from the dead, the empty tomb is a first step through which the disciples could begin to understand the significance of Christ's resurrection. A "young man" in radiant clothing, identified as an angel in St. Matthew's account (28:2), announces the message that Christ has died and risen. The empty tomb is, as the *Catechism of the Catholic Church* notes, "an essential sign" for this announcement: "He has risen, he is not here; see the place where they laid him" (*Catechism*, 640, Mk 16:6).

The empty tomb offers a trustworthy historical testimony to Christ's rising from the dead. It prevents us from concluding that the Resurrection was purely a "spiritual" event or a metaphor. At the same time, this sign reminds us that Christ's resurrection transcends history. The deeper significance of this event requires faith, because Christ's resurrection is far more than simply the restoration of human life. The Resurrection is not simply a *resuscitation*, in which a dead body regains the life that it had before. Rather, Christ rises to a fuller and more perfect form of life which is no longer subject to death.

In light of this transcendent message, we can understand why knowledge of the Resurrection requires faith in God's chosen *witnesses*. The Gospels offer unanimous testimony that the first of these witnesses were women. While not explicitly mentioned by the Evangelists, Christian piety recognizes that the Blessed Virgin Mary would have been the first witness to the Resurrection. The broader announcement of the Resurrection begins with the holy women who come to the tomb to anoint Jesus' body. In this way, Christ's resurrection brings about a renewed awareness of the dignity of women. Their testimony is no longer to be held unreliable, as it had been in Jewish tradition. As St. Bede points out, "as woman was the first to taste death, so woman was the first to witness the Resurrection."

The renewal brought about by the risen Christ extends also to the apostles and especially Peter. In spite of their betrayals, the Resurrection restores their leadership and establishes them as authoritative witnesses of Christ's rising. While not the only witnesses of this event, their particular closeness to Christ in his earthly life and resurrection makes them the most important witnesses to the truth of Christ's victory over death. In spite of their continued disbelief, they see firsthand the risen body of Christ and receive Jesus' command to announce this message (Lk 24:39–40). They see firsthand the wounds still present in the risen Christ, which manifest the continuity between Christ's death and the resurrected body (Jn 20:24–27). St. Paul would later experience an appearance of the risen Christ and come to share in the authority of the apostles (1 Cor 15:8–10).

The multitude of witnesses firmly establishes the truth of Christ's resurrection at a historical level. Faith, moved by God's grace, leads the disciples to recognize this event as the great manifestation of God's power. Through the Resurrection, Christ does not simply work a miracle, but brings about a radical renewal of creation. Only God can bring life to the dead and exalt Christ in glory. The risen Christ "lives by the power of God" (2 Cor 13:4), and through this power he is "designated Son of God in power according to the Spirit of holiness by his resurrection from the dead" (Rom 1:4).

Faith allows us to perceive that, beyond the historical fact of the event, the Resurrection is a fulfillment and completion of the entire history of salvation. Through the resurrection of Christ, God carries out the Redemption from sin which has afflicted human history from its origins. In this transcendent action, God reveals that the sacrifice made by Christ on the Cross has been a fully acceptable and satisfactory oblation. Moreover, through the raising up of Christ, God the Father shows his definitive approval of the entire meaning of Christ's life, which otherwise might have seemed to end in a humiliating death.

Since the Resurrection was such an unprecedented and unexpected event, the early Church sought for the adequate means to explain this occurrence. Although the Resurrection will always remain a profound mystery, the Church would gradually find in the Scriptures, through grace, a language for expressing this truth. As we have noted, St. Mark particularly expresses the sense of surprise and confusion experienced by the disciples when they first encountered the empty tomb. The Gospels of Matthew and Luke, on the other hand, show more awareness of how the Resurrection fits into God's plan.

Matthew's description of the dead who come out of their graves (27:51–53) seems to show the fulfillment of Ezekiel's prophecy of resurrection, in which God promises to his people that "I will open your graves, and raise you from your graves" (Ez 37:12). With these events, Matthew shows that Christ's death and resurrection have brought about the new age of the Messiah. Christ's parting words, in which he proclaims that "All authority in heaven and on earth has been given to me"(Mt 28:18). show that the kingdom of the Messiah has now been inaugurated.

St. Luke, in chapter twenty-four of his Gospel, offers some more details about the process through which the disciples come to appreciate the meaning of the Resurrection. The Evangelist strongly accentuates the physicality of the risen Christ, who can be touched and is able to eat. Through their contact with the glorious body, the disciples experience a profound renewal in their minds. After his appearance to the apostles, Jesus "opened their minds to understand the scriptures" (verse 45). In this manner, Christ explains that his death and resurrection were foretold in the "the law of Moses and the prophets and the psalms" (verse 44). The story of the disciples of Emmaus further shows the radical new perspective on Scripture which Christ opens up, which becomes the source of the interior zeal which needs to drive Christians (verse 32). Luke shows that Christ's resurrection is the fulfillment of Jewish expectations, but he also has in mind a universal horizon. Jesus goes on to announce that "repentance and forgiveness of sins should be preached in his name to all nations, beginning from Jerusalem" (verse 47).

The last of the Gospels to be composed, St. John's, is the most suffused with the glory of Christ's triumph over death. The New Testament scholar N. T. Wright considers the Resurrection to be the eighth of the signs described in John's Gospel, through which Christ reveals his glory. The seventh of these signs, in Wright's view, is the Crucifixion, which brings to completion the old creation which took seven days. With this eighth sign, a new creation shines forth.

In the same Gospel, Christ is the new temple who brings to fulfillment the worship of the Old Law (see Jn 2:19–22). The gift of the Holy Spirit, promised throughout the Gospel and offered by the risen Christ, is the "breath" of God's life which recreates man (Jn 20:22). This 'breath' echoes the original breath by which God had first created man in his image (see Gn 2:7).

St. John manifests the glory of the risen Christ, but also offers a vivid portrayal of the path of faith through which we come to appreciate the truth of Easter. The apostle Thomas' confession of Christ as "My Lord and my God!" (20:28) is the culminating moment in the drama of unbelief and faith which runs throughout the Gospel. With these words pronounced in the presence of the risen Christ and his glorious humanity, Thomas recognizes that Christ is both God and the Messiah, Israel's expected king.

The Gospel accounts, along with the other New Testament writings, allow us to grasp the way the early Church matured from the shock of Easter morning to an understanding of the Resurrection as the climax of God's plan of salvation. From the first public announcement of this glorious event at Pentecost, the Church confidently proclaims that the Resurrection is the fulfillment of the promises made in the Hebrew Scriptures. Christ's resurrection manifests that he is the king, foretold by David, who would be exalted at the right hand of the Father (see Acts 2:34, 13:32–33, Ps 2:7, 110:1). Christ is the servant of Yahweh, who has been exalted by God after his redemptive sufferings (see Acts 4:30; Phil 2:7; Is 53:11). As we have seen, he is the new Adam as well as the holy one, announced in the psalm, who would not experience corruption. Christ is the kingly figure, announced in Psalm 118, who has fought a fierce battle against his enemies and emerged victorious by the power of God (see Acts 4:11). This king, articulating his experience of distress and liberation, describes himself as a stone: "The stone which the builders rejected has become the head of the corner" (verse 22).

With this language, the Church expressed the great message which brings fulfillment to the hope of Israel and to all of humanity: Christ truly has risen from the dead, and this resurrection stands at the center of salvation history. With this event, God has accomplished the definitive victory over sin and death.

C. The Glorification of Christ as a Result of His Passion

Having discussed the truth of Christ's resurrection and its significance in God's plan, we can now examine some further issues regarding the meaning of this event. In the first place, we should appreciate that while Christ's death brings about our redemption, the Resurrection is not an event that occurs "after" the Redemption. Rather, the Resurrection is an essential part of the Redemption, along with Christ's suffering and death. All of these events are part of one single reality, the paschal mystery, through which God carries out our salvation.

Christ's suffering and death might seem to be diametrically opposed to his resurrection. Nevertheless, St. Paul asserts that God glorifies Christ precisely because of Christ's obedience on the Cross (Phil 2:8–9). As we have seen, Christ's passion demonstrates, in a supreme way, the obedience and love which merit salvation for the human race. As a consequence, Christ's suffering itself bears the mark of God's glory. From this perspective, St. John depicts Christ's death as a moment of glorification (Jn 12:23). On the other hand, after this death the risen and glorified Christ still bears the marks of his passion (Jn 20:25–27).

The Cross and the Resurrection mutually illuminate the mystery of salvation, as indicated by St. Paul's statement that Christ was "put to death for our trespasses and raised for our justification" (Rom 4:25). In light of this text and the overall mystery revealed in Scripture, St. Thomas Aquinas points out that Christ's passion is the cause of the forgiveness of sins. The Resurrection, he asserts, is the cause of the new life given to us by the risen Christ. This "new life" refers to both the participation in the divine life which the Christian experiences through grace, and to the future resurrection of the body.

The intertwined roles of Christ's death and resurrection show us how Christ's paschal mystery is the definitive "*pass over*." With his death, Christ takes up the sins of the world and in his resurrection we see the beginning of a renewed world, purified of sin. The risen body of Christ is the visible manifestation of this new creation, through which God intends to renew all of humanity.

St. Paul describes the risen body of Christ as "a spiritual body" (1 Cor 15:44). As the Resurrection appearances show, Christ's body is a real body with physical properties. At the same time, it is not simply a "physical body" (1 Cor 15:44), that is, a body with the ordinary human condition. The risen Christ is no longer subject to the limits of space and time. He passes through the room in which "the doors were shut" so as to manifest his humanity to the disciples and later Thomas (Jn 20:19, 26). Christ is no longer subject to a determined physical appearance, and at times he cannot be recognized by those who knew him well (Jn 20:14, 21:4).

These properties of the risen Christ do not indicate a lack of humanity, but rather reveal a humanity which has become fully penetrated with God. By the very fact of taking on a human nature at his conception, Christ was and is always fully God. Still, in the Resurrection the full consequences of this union of the divine and human are revealed. In his resurrected body, Christ's humanity has been fully taken up into the life of God. This real body is entirely subject to the will of God and, while present on earth, totally belongs to heaven. As a result, the *Catechism of the Catholic Church* points out that "the risen Jesus enjoys the sovereign freedom of appearing as he wishes" (645).

The characteristics of Christ's risen humanity make it clear that Christ's resurrection is not akin to a return to earthly life, as in the case of Lazarus or the son of the widow of Nain (Jn 11:44; Lk 7:15). Christ has risen to a new and glorious life in which his body "is filled with the power of the Holy Spirit: he shares the divine life in his glorious state, so that St. Paul can say that Christ is 'the man of heaven'" (*Catechism*, 645; see 1 Cor 1:35–50).

This taking up of Christ's humanity into the Spirit's power does not mean that Christ's humanity is taken away or absorbed by the divinity. Rather, the Trinity fully transforms the human nature of Christ so that this human nature, as Michael Schmaus asserts, "becomes the representation and showing forth of God's glory; the divine glory becomes accessible and perceptible in it, and the eye which is clear of sight is able to see the glory of God in the human nature of Jesus."

As God is love (1 Jn 4:7), and the Spirit of God is a Spirit of love (Rom 5:5), the risen Christ manifests God's *love* in a particular way. The risen Christ reaches out in charity to Mary Magdalene, the disciples at Emmaus, and the apostles. He offers to the apostles the Holy Spirit, which is the outpouring of God's love to man (Jn 20:22). He walks alongside the disciples of Emmaus and, overlooking their initial harsh response, accompanies them in their discouragement (Lk 24:18–27). He has compassion upon the initial unbelief of the apostles and especially Thomas, and even prepares breakfast for them (Jn 21:12).

In all of these appearances, the risen Christ communicates the full meaning of the Redemption. As St. Paul indicates, without the Resurrection something essential for our salvation would be missing: "If Christ has not been raised, your faith is futile and you are still in your sins" (1 Cor 15:17). Apart from being the definitive proof of the truth of Christ's mission, the risen Christ is a tangible reminder that sin has been defeated. While Christ was always without sin, his risen body shows that the limitations to human nature due to sin—suffering and death—have been eliminated in him.

From this perspective we can see how the resurrection of Christ, while an event which applies in a special way to the Son of God alone, is an essential cause of salvation and sign of hope for all humanity. Although it was an indescribable event which occurred in the life of one person, like the mustard seed its effect expands far beyond this origin. Though only a select group of persons witnessed the event, in the Resurrection—as Joseph Ratzinger affirms—"a new possibility of human existence is attained that affects everyone and that opens up a future, a new kind of future, for mankind." Christ's appearance as a gardener reminds us that in him, the original Garden of Eden has been restored and re-created. Christ is the "the first fruits" (1 Cor 15:23) of the new humanity, free of sin and filled with grace, which God desires to bring about. He offers the promise that the disorders in our present condition, due to sin, can be healed and transformed by God's grace.

Significantly, the theme of hope is not directly present in the actual Resurrection narratives recorded in the Gospels. This phenomenon is a reminder that the Resurrection accounts narrate real events and were not simply written to console the early Christians. Rather, the early Church came to interpret the event of the Resurrection, with the grace of the Holy Spirit, as having its profound meaning.

Of course, in addition to the actual narratives of the Resurrection, other New Testament writings give powerful expression to the meaning of the Resurrection for the Christian life. The reality of Christ's rising from the dead gives full significance to baptism, the essential rite of Christian initiation. In this sacrament, the immersion in water mystically incorporates the believer into Christ's death and also makes him a participant in Christ's resurrection. As St. Paul states, "We were buried therefore with him by baptism into death, so that as Christ was raised from the dead by the glory of the Father, we too might walk in newness of life" (Rom 6:4).

Christ's resurrection is the sign of a new life of grace, through which in the present life the believer shares in the divine life. With regard to this state, resurrection serves as a metaphor for the life of grace which gives the believer a genuine supernatural life. At the same time, this metaphor of spiritual resurrection depends on the literal resurrection of the dead which believers await. The newness of Christian life, through which the believer breaks with sin and lives as a son of God, is the pathway toward the resurrection of the body in the life to come. As the Apostle of the Gentiles comments in the Letter to the Romans, the new life of grace leads believers to look forward to "the redemption of our bodies" (8:23), a phrase which implies the resurrection of the dead.

Hence, while possessing the fruits of the Resurrection through grace, Christians eagerly await the fullness of the Resurrection in their own bodies. As St. Paul states in his letter to the Corinthians, Christ's resurrection is the cause of the future resurrection of believers: "For as by a man came death, by a man has come also the resurrection of the dead. For as in Adam all die, so also in Christ shall all be made alive" (1 Cor 15:21–22).

This resurrection, like that of Christ, is not simply a return to the state of being alive, but implies a conformation to Christ's glorious and risen state. Christ will "will change our lowly body to be like his glorious body" (Phil 3:21). Here, we see how Christ's resurrection unveils the glorious splendor to which the human being, created in the image and likeness of God, is called.

D. The Ascension

The Resurrection, as we have seen, reveals Christ's decisive triumph over sin. At the same time, in the appearances of the risen Christ, the glory of this victory remains hidden within an ordinary human appearance. Christ has inaugurated a kingdom which is not of this world (Jn 18:36). His true glory, the glory he had "before the world was made" (Jn 17:5), lies in his eternal communion with the Father.

In his manifestations after the Resurrection, Christ exists in a kind of intermediate state between earth and heaven. He is present on the earth and, as he tells Mary Magdalene, he has "not yet ascended to the Father" (Jn 20:17). Even so, Christ's humanity is in a new state. The Gospels do not recount that he had an earthly habitation after the Resurrection, which leads us to suppose that his home is heaven. Christ's words in his resurrection appearances seem to indicate that he is in a transitory state. He has been gloriously exalted by the Father, and yet he has not yet fully entered into his definitive communion with the Father in heaven.

With his *ascension*, Christ makes this complete entrance into a glorious and exalted state. The Gospels recount Christ being raised into heaven, which in biblical language is synonymous with entering fully into the life of God (Mk 16:19 and Lk 24:51).

From the moment of his resurrection, Christ is already fully glorified. From the point of view of Christ himself, the Ascension simply *manifests* the glory which remained hidden in Christ's risen humanity. In addition, the Ascension involves an *exaltation* by which Christ receives dominion over all creation.

This exaltation reveals more completely to mankind the full significance of Christ's earthly life as a manifestation of God's own life. In being lifted up to the glory of heaven, as Thomas Aquinas states, Christ opens up the path for believers to enter heaven. As in all the events of Christ's life, the conclusion of Christ's earthly life manifests the final end, in God, to which every human being is called.

While the risen Christ needed to appear to the disciples for their instruction, Christ's true home is in heaven and not in a fallen world. After making the command to preach the Gospel to all nations, Jesus was taken up to heaven "and sat down at the right hand of God" (Mk 16:19). This image of being seated "at the right hand" shows Christ as the fulfillment of the kingly figure presented in Psalm 110. In this psalm, the king occupies a special place of honor at the right hand of God, which ensures the king's victory.

From this royal perspective, the Ascension involves an enthronement in which Christ assumes the role of king of all creation. In heaven, Christ receives praise and homage from the heavenly court and all creatures (Rv 5:11–13). St. Paul specifies that Christ's lordship over creation will only be fully realized at the end of time, "[w]hen all things are subjected to him" and Christ in turn will offer all creation to the Father (1 Cor 15:28).

The Ascension marks the end of Christ's earthly life among us, and at the same time the beginning of a new mode of presence in the world. From heaven, Christ continues his role of priestly, prophetic, and royal mediation before the Father on our behalf (Heb 7:24–25). He exercises and extends his lordship, through the power of the Holy Spirit, until it reaches its final realization. This action of spreading the fruits of the Resurrection, through the Church, will be the subject of the next chapter.

E. The Exaltation of Christ and the Redemptive Meaning of Suffering

Christ's resurrection, as we have seen, gives a radically new meaning to his suffering on the Cross. With the glorification of Christ after his passion, God also gives a new sense to all the afflictions which affect human life.

As much as medical care has developed in the last centuries, the problem of suffering continues to be an acute one in our culture. In a world which often exalts pleasure and material comfort, many people would like to think that the reality of pain might simply be eliminated. However, we know that suffering and pain continue to exist and bring not simply physical difficulty but also psychological and spiritual distress.

Scripture reminds us that physical suffering, however challenging it might for us, is the consequence of a much deeper suffering, which is that which exists in the human soul. The true and definitive suffering for human beings is the total absence of God. While in physical pain our natural desire for well-being is thwarted, in sin we go against our deepest desire for fulfillment and happiness in God. From this perspective, damnation is the definitive suffering we face. While the New Testament uses the image of physical suffering to describe the pains of hell, the greatest suffering of this state is that of freely rejecting communion with God.

Physical suffering, therefore, serves as a reminder of the fallen condition of humanity and the necessity of the redemption. In this aspect of life, as in all the dimensions of human existence, we stands in need of the salvific mediation of Christ.

Christ, while remaining without sin, has fully taken on the reality of human suffering. Jesus Christ, who had a true human nature, really did experience pain. The Church has had to affirm this truth in the face of those who thought that it was unworthy that God should have a real body and suffer. In the early centuries after Christ, the Docetists denied that Christ had a real body; the Monophysites held that the divine nature absorbed the human nature, and as a result Christ would not suffer.

If Jesus suffered, does this mean that God can suffer? In the strict sense, no. God is completely transcendent to the reality of suffering. In himself, God is full of perfection and infinite bliss. However, in Christ, the Second Person of the Trinity has taken on a human nature and has willed to take on the human reality of suffering.

In his human nature, Christ suffers in both body and soul. This human nature is united to the divine nature in the Person of the Incarnate Word. Consequently, because of the hypostatic union, we can say that in the case of Christ God is the subject of suffering. Still, the suffering itself occurs in the human rather than the divine nature.

While we should always keep in mind the reality that God is transcendent, the mystery of Christ's suffering reveals to us the extent to which God has associated himself with human suffering. Jesus experiences the greatest humiliation and pain in his human nature. Because this human nature is that of the divine Person of the Son, this suffering is—as St. John Paul II affirmed—of "an incomparable depth and intensity."

The Son of God's suffering out of love transforms the human reality of suffering. Suffering, through the Cross and Resurrection, becomes linked with glory. As the risen Christ asks the disciples at Emmaus, "Was it not necessary that the Christ should suffer these things and enter into his glory?" (Lk 24:26). The Resurrection and Exaltation of Christ reveal that Jesus' sufferings are in fact the manifestation of his glory as the Messiah.

This glory reveals the glory which can be present in our suffering, if we open our hearts to the mystery of the Redemption. Suffering in light of Christ becomes, as John Paul II observed, "an invitation to manifest the moral greatness of man, his spiritual maturity." Through Christ's passion, each person is called to accept and even embrace the afflictions of human life, as a means of sharing in the redemptive suffering of Christ. Through this suffering united to Christ by the power of the Holy Spirit, the infinite power of the Redemption reaches humanity through the mystery of the Church. Pain, instead of being a source of sadness, becomes for the Christian a means—as St. Josemaría Escrivá states—to "follow in the footsteps of Christ, with a zeal to co-redeem all mankind."

CHAPTER 10

The Lordship of Christ

> Since Jesus has reascended into heaven, I can follow Him only in the traces He has left; but how luminous these traces are! how perfumed! I have only to cast a glance in the Gospels and immediately I breathe in the perfumes of Jesus' life, and I know on which side to run.
>
> —*St. Thérèse of Lisieux*

A. Redemption in Christ and the Sending of the Holy Spirit

The Holy Spirit is intimately involved in the entire existence and redemptive mission of Christ. As we have seen, the Holy Spirit's action brings about the Incarnation of the Son of God in the womb of the Blessed Virgin. Christ offers his perfect sacrifice on the Cross "through the eternal Spirit" (Heb 9:14). Christ's resurrection brings about a new stage in God's plan in which this same Spirit is now offered to us as gift.

The Holy Spirit is given to us as a fruit of Christ's passion and death. St. John, in particular, emphasizes that Christ's sacrifice on the Cross is the necessary condition for this gift. Before this moment, "the Spirit had not been given, because Jesus was not yet glorified" (Jn 7:39). At the Last Supper, Jesus makes it clear that if he does not depart, the Holy Spirit will not come to the apostles (Jn 16:7).

From these texts, we can appreciate that the Redemption accomplished by Christ is communicated to us through the

Holy Spirit. The Holy Spirit molds and shapes each person into the divine image which God desires for us, in a way similar to that action by which the Holy Spirit fills and shapes the sacred humanity of Christ.

The Spirit's special role in bringing Christ's redemption to humanity is in keeping with the particular role of the Holy Spirit within the Trinity. Within the life of the Trinity, the Holy Spirit proceeds from the Father and the Son; the third Person of the Trinity is the mutual love of the Father and the Son. The Holy Spirit, as a divine Person, manifests to us the perfection with which the Father and Son love one another.

In God's plan of creation and salvation, the gift of the Holy Spirit also signifies perfection, in the sense of the perfect completion of God's saving love. Christ's perfect giving of himself in love, on the Cross, is the source of a new gift of love which is the Holy Spirit. As St. John Paul II taught in his encyclical on the Third Person of the Trinity: "The gift made by the Son completes the revelation and giving of the eternal love: the Holy Spirit, who in the inscrutable depths of the divinity is a Person-Gift."

Here, we can see how the Holy Spirit forms an essential part of the mystery of Christ's redemption. The risen Christ offers the apostles the Holy Spirit, who communicates the forgiveness of sins which Christ has accomplished with his redemptive death (Jn 20:22–23). This gift of the risen Christ marks a new age in salvation history, as John Paul II further states: a "new beginning of the self-communication of the Triune God."

At *Pentecost*, the same Spirit who descended upon the Blessed Virgin, to bring about the Incarnation of the Son of God, now descends upon humanity in a public way and on a grand scale.

Pentecost was originally the Jewish feast, connected with the Passover, in which the first fruits of the harvest were offered to God. Later, the feast was linked with the giving of the Law at Mount Sinai, and was fixed at the date fifty days after Passover. In this way, the feast brought together two aspects of our duty to glorify God: first, that of offering him the first fruits of our work; secondly, his duty to worship God through the Law. While the Feast of Passover recalls the miraculous action of God through which the Chosen People are given freedom, Pentecost points in a particular way toward the response of adoration by which we respond to God's action.

At the Christian Pentecost, fifty days after the resurrection of Christ, the Jewish feast of Pentecost comes to its fulfillment. At this moment in which the Jews would typically collect the fruits of the harvest, the first disciples receive the great fruit of Christ's death on the Cross, which is the Holy Spirit. This Spirit in turn enables us to offer the true worship of which the earlier rites and the Law were simply a figure.

Through the descent of the Spirit, God brings to completion various promises of the Old Testament. In the face of the Chosen People's experience of sin and desolation, God had pledged to cleanse them of sin and put "a new heart" and "a new spirit" within them (Ez 36:26). Through these gifts, God foretells that his people will be empowered to walk in his statutes and become careful to observe his ordinances (Ez 36:27). The Spirit would no longer be solely identified with the messiah or with a few select persons. As foretold by the Old Testament, the Spirit would become the possession of all in the messianic kingdom (Jl 2:28). The entire people would become prophets who announce and teach the mystery of God (Jl 2:28–29; Jer 31:34).

The signs which accompany the descent of the Holy Spirit at Pentecost reveal that the new age of the Messiah has arrived. A mighty wind and tongues of fire, both signs of God's presence in the Old Testament, come down upon all of the disciples and lead them to prophesy (Acts 2:1–4). St. Peter announces that the pouring out of the Spirit, promised by God through the prophet Joel, has now come about (Acts 2:16–21). He proceeds to proclaim, for the first time in a public way, the message of Christ's death and resurrection. Peter goes on to affirm the need for baptism, so that his hearers and all of humanity might receive the fruits of salvation in Christ.

In this scene, we can see the profound relationship between the events of Easter and Pentecost. In the early centuries of the Church, Pentecost referred to the entire Easter season, which commemorated the Resurrection, Ascension, and Descent of the Holy Spirit, as well as the entire Christian mystery. At the first Christian Pentecost, believers begin to participate, even if in a limited way, in the glorious transformation of humanity accomplished in the risen Christ. As St. Josemaría Escrivá comments in his homily for this feast, the minds and hearts of believers are opened to "a new light"; the Spirit purifies them of their earlier weaknesses and makes them "firm, strong, daring."

This new life given to believers, and offered to all humanity, will only come to its full realization at the end of time. St. Paul, as he describes the life of divine sonship which Christians experience in the present life, invites believers to look forward to a greater life in which the Holy Spirit will transform the body of believers according to the model of Christ's glorious body: "If the Spirit of him who raised Jesus from the dead dwells in you, he who raised Christ Jesus from the dead will give life to your mortal bodies also through his Spirit which dwells in you." (Rom 8:11).

Pentecost reveals more clearly that the redemption carried out by Christ is the work of the entire Trinity. All of the three divine Persons are at work in the Redemption, and each one acts in accord with his own specific mode of being within the Trinity. The Father sends the Son for the redemption of man, and glorifies the Son in response to the Son's total offering of himself upon the Cross. This action of the Father and the Son take place within the unity of the Holy Spirit. The Holy Spirit is at work throughout the mission of Christ, who acts in the power of the Spirit, and the Holy Spirit is constantly at work in bringing the gift of the Redemption to the human person. This saving action of the Trinity in us gives rise to the mystery of the Church, which will be our next topic of study.

B. God's Salvific Action in the Church

The gift of the Holy Spirit transforms man and brings about the new community of the *Church*. St. Paul describe the Church as the *pleroma* or fullness of Christ (Eph 1:23). This term indicates that the Church shares in the fullness of salvation which has been given to Christ.

Christ himself is the place in which the "fulness of God" dwells (Col 1:19). At the same time, God's presence in Christ is the principle and source of God's desire to extend this presence to all of humanity. As the ecclesiology specialist María del Pilar Río points out, the New Testament reveals the Church to be the fulfillment of God's Old Testament promise to make his dwelling place with his people (see Ez 37:27; 2 Cor 6:16). This pledge, she notes, does not refer simply to a vague presence but includes God's desire to raise the Christian to the level of being a son of God, in keeping with God's promise to be a father to the messiah (see 2 Sm 7:14).

Through the gift of the Holy Spirit, the Church is the special site in which God makes himself present among humanity. The gift of tongues at Pentecost indicates that this community of the Church, while being composed of a limited number of people, is called to extend to all of mankind.

After Christ's ascension into heaven, the Church continues Christ's presence in the world. The Fathers of the Church appreciated that, just as Eve was born from the side of Adam while asleep, the Church was born from Christ's side in the "sleep" of death. In the blood and water which spring forth from this side, we can see an image for the sacrifice of Christ and the gift of the Spirit which give life to the Church. As we have seen, the blood and water also serve as signs for the sacraments of the Eucharist and baptism, efficacious signs through which God bestows supernatural life upon us.

By virtue of the action of Christ and the Holy Spirit, the Church is the *Mystical Body* of Christ. By means of her, the risen Christ lives on and continues to offer the gift of the Paraclete.

While the Church is not the same as Jesus' actual physical body, the Church's identity as Body of Christ is not simply a metaphor. The union of Christ with the Church is called *mystical* to distinguish it from the physical body of Christ, but also to indicate a real though mysterious supernatural bond. The Holy Spirit, the soul of the Mystical Body, gives life to the members of the Church and unites them in charity to Christ, the Head of the Body.

This activity of the Holy Spirit truly transforms believers and makes them, through the Church—as the French New Testament scholar Fernand Prat noted—"an extension of Christ in time and space." The identification between Christ and the Church is so profound that, as Christ indicates to St. Paul in the moment of his conversion, Paul's persecution of the Church is a persecution of Jesus (Acts 9:5).

The Apostle's use of the term *pleroma,* in relation to the Church, further signifies that the Mystical Body of Christ is the *complement* of the person of Christ. Christ is the realization of the Father's eternal plan to raise all human beings to the divine life. God wills him to be "the first-born among many brethren" (Rom 8:29). As the New Adam—as we have seen in chapter seven—Christ is a representative for all persons.

From this perspective, we can appreciate how the Church is an essential "completion" of Christ, just as the body is a necessary completion of the head. God has bestowed the fullness of grace on Christ so that Christ in turn might pass on this grace to the Church and, through the Church, to all humanity. In light of this truth, St. Augustine speaks of Christ and the Church as together making up the "whole Christ" (*Christus totus*).

In the mystery of the Church, we see how the risen Christ, ascended to the glory of heaven, continues to act and distribute the gift of salvation to humanity. This mystery also shows how salvation itself involves a profound identification with Christ himself. In baptism, the believer is incorporated mystically into the life of Christ and becomes a new creature in him. God intends this identification to grow through confirmation, the Holy Eucharist, and in the myriad facets of the Christian life.

The Christian, freely responding to the gift of grace, is called to be a continuation of Christ's presence. We have the vocation to be not just *like* Christ, but through the reality of the Mystical Body, to *be* Christ. Such is the genuine implication of the profound reality of the Church, as St. Josemaría Escrivá affirms: "Embracing the Christian faith means committing oneself to continuing Jesus Christ's mission among men. We must, each of us, be *alter Christus, ipse Christus*: another Christ, Christ himself."

The Christological dimension of salvation helps us to appreciate in a more tangible manner just what *salvation* and *redemption* mean. As discussed in chapter one, people of all times have recognized the need for liberation from the moral and metaphysical evils which afflict the human condition in its fallen state. As the Second Vatican Council stated in the Constitution *Gaudium et Spes*: "Christ, the final Adam, by the revelation of the mystery of the Father and His love, fully reveals man to man himself and makes his supreme calling clear."

Christ reveals the plan which God had for man and woman when he created them in his image and likeness. Every instant of the life of Christ, as we have seen, manifests the will of God for each person. Each of these moments is a mystery of salvation. All of these circumstances have a divine meaning through the Incarnation, and they are all glorified in the Resurrection. As a result, all of the moments of Christ's earthly life remain eternally assumed in the risen Christ. Ascended into heaven and exalted by the Father, the glorified Christ can communicate to us the divine grace and deep human meaning present in every aspect of our lives.

Through this action, perceptible only to the eyes of faith, Christ pours out the graces of salvation upon us and upon all human realities, so that creation might be conformed to God's plan. In the midst of the vicissitudes of history and proliferation of sin, the mystery of salvation is at work in the Mystical Body of Christ. As Vatican II's *Constitution on the Church* stated: "The Church, or, in other words, the kingdom of Christ now present in mystery, grows visibly through the power of God in the world."

C. Redemption as Liberation from Slavery to Sin, to the Devil, and to Death

Christians, while awaiting the fullness of redemption in the age to come, already experience now, in the present life, an authentic experience of liberation. From the early centuries the Church realized that the emancipation of the Chosen People from slavery in Egypt is a figure of a deeper liberation, which has been brought about by Jesus Christ's death and resurrection. Christ redeems us from the slavery of *sin* and offers us true freedom (see Jn 8:34–36).

We have seen how Christ's perfect offering of himself makes superabundant atonement to God for all the sins of mankind.

Christ's death has the power of eliminating the stain of sin and destroying its power over us (see 1 Jn 3:8–9).

In light of this truth of faith, we might reasonably ask, How does this liberation take place? If we believers are truly freed from sin, why must we still struggle against the "the lust of the flesh and the lust of the eyes and the pride of life" (1 Jn 2:16)?

The Council of Trent responded to this question in its description of the gift of Redemption. Following the teaching of the New Testament, the Council affirmed that baptism brings about a genuine transformation from a state of sin to a new life in Christ. The Council recognized that concupiscence, or the inclination to sin, remains in the baptized. Still, the presence of this sinful tendency serves as an occasion for the more powerful action of grace.

The inclination to sin, though "it is left for us to wrestle with," "cannot injure those who do not acquiesce but resist manfully by the grace of Jesus Christ." The Council Fathers here make reference to St. Paul's admonition to Timothy: "An athlete is not crowned unless he competes according to the rules" (2 Tm 2:5). In other words, the presence of sin is an opportunity for the Christian to freely reject sin through the power of grace. In this manner, we have a real participation in the victory over sin which Christ has won.

The New Testament bears continual witness to the genuine, though imperfect, quality of the liberation experienced by the Christian. The human intellect is freed from ignorance and receives a new light so as to know God and his plans (see Rom 12:2). The human will receives a new strength to reject sin and live in holiness (see Rom 6:17). Disordered passions no longer have dominion over human action (see Eph 2:3–7).

Along with the liberation from sin, we are freed from the power of the *devil*. Sin is a human act in which we freely choose to reject God's will. At the same time, Scripture shows that from the beginning of human history and throughout history, the devil continually seeks to incite us to disobey God. As in the case of the temptations that Christ experiences in the desert, Satan seeks to lead us to distrust God and seek fulfillment apart from our Creator. With original sin, man falls prey to the devil and, without grace, we remain subject to the devil's influence.

The coming of the Son of God in the flesh has led to the definitive defeat of the devil. Christ manifests this triumph in his expulsion of demons, which reveals that the kingdom of God has entered into human history (see Mt 22:28). With Christ's death, Satan is "cast out" and creation is restored to God's plan through Christ (see Jn 12:31–32).

In no way does the New Testament imply that Christ's victory ends the action of the devil in history. In fact, the Book of Revelation warns us that the devil, while being cast out from heaven, acts all the more ferociously on earth: "[W]oe to you, O earth and sea, for the devil has come down to you in great wrath, because he knows that his time is short!" (Rv 12:12). Nonetheless, Christians can act serenely amidst this reality, with the certainty that the devil has no power over Christ (see Jn 14:30). Christians share in this victory over the devil; through grace Christ "has delivered us from the dominion of darkness and transferred us to the kingdom of his beloved Son" (Col 1:13).

The totality of Christ's triumph is shown in particular in the liberation from *death*. Death is the last and the culminating punishment which God pronounces for the first sin (Gn 3:19). As much as our society might try to ignore or deny it, death remains the inescapable and tangible sign of our limits and our need for salvation. It continues to be a source of anxiety and sadness, as many are tormented by the deterioration of their bodies and the fear of being eliminated forever.

Christ, through his death, has taken on the sorrows of death and transformed them. As St. Paul affirms, "Christ being raised from the dead will never die again; death no longer has dominion over him" (Rom 6:9). Christians live in the hope that, with the final resurrection of the body, they will share in this conclusive victory over death. Even in the present life, through a life of faith, hope, and love, believers are freed from the *fear of death* which plagues so many of our contemporaries (see Heb 2:14–15).

In light of Christ's death and resurrection, the human reality of death is not erased, but it does take on a new meaning. Through grace, death becomes an occasion through which the disciples of Jesus can definitively offer themselves to God, in union with Christ's perfect sacrifice. The Christian lives with confidence that, as in the case of Christ's death, death becomes a moment for a final glorification. Death is no longer a loss, but the path to a new and eternal inheritance for Christians, who have been made "heirs of God and fellow heirs with Christ" (Rom 8:17).

The radical freedom brought about by Christ can be summarized as a freedom to *love*. As Jutta Burggraf points out, "love is the key to freedom." Love, she notes, allows for a renewed vision of the world which goes beyond the limited horizons left by sin. Love also allows for a true interior freedom by which we can participate in God's own charity.

The freedom offered in Christ is, in the first place, a freedom offered to each individual *person*. Christ has redeemed all of humanity, but God respects the liberty of each person to accept or reject the gift of salvation.

The Christian message of freedom, based on the immense dignity of each person, has and continues to be a positive force for social improvement. At the same time, in past decades, many have presented this liberation in a way which deforms its authentic meaning. Such has been the case in some so-called theologies of liberation, which contain Christian elements within a Marxist ideology. In such theologies, liberation would come about not through the action of grace within the human heart but rather by a class struggle in which the poor would be "liberated" by political revolution.

The temptation to empty the true meaning of Christian liberation is not just limited to such radical ideologies. In the face of the pressing injustices in the world, we can be easily led to look for a "salvation" which would be simply temporal. Within such a perspective, the "spiritual" elements of liberation would seem to be less urgent.

In light of these various attempts to turn Christian freedom into a liberation at the purely temporal level, the Christian faith reminds us that the deepest bondage is that present within the human heart. The Second Vatican Council's Constitution *Gaudium et Spes* notes that along with the sin which marks man's origins, "examining his heart, man finds that he has inclinations toward evil too, and is engulfed by manifold ills which cannot come from his good Creator." This disorder, present in the human heart due to sin, is the ultimate source of the many other maladies which afflict our lives, our relationships with others, and our connection with all creation.

True liberation can only come from the Holy Spirit, who works in the heart of each person to make present Christ's redemption. The Paraclete's saving action frees the Christian from sin, so as to live "the glorious liberty of the children of God" (Rom 8:21). This freedom, while present in the human heart, is not simply "personal." The grace of God refashions the human heart according to supernatural charity, and leads it outward to transform the world in the spirit of Christ.

As Pope Francis states in his exhortation *Joy of the Gospel*, "an authentic faith—which is never comfortable or completely personal—always involves a deep desire to change the world, to transmit values, to leave this earth somehow better than we found it." While Christian liberation remains always directed toward personal communion with God, this same communion is born and grows within a *community* of persons. Christians, especially the laity who are immersed in the daily realities of the world, have the call and duty to fill institutions, laws, and all of society with the spirit of the Gospel. In this manner, the Christian helps to see—in the words of St. Josemaría Escrivá—"Christ's love and freedom preside over all aspects of modern life," and in this way we contribute to bringing about the authentic liberation which the human heart longs for.

D. The Second Coming of Christ

Through the mystery of the Church, as we have seen, Christ exercises his loving dominion in a way which respects our freedom. In a way which is *fortiter et suaviter*—"strong and gentle," as the Book of Wisdom describes God's action (see Wis 8:1, Latin Vulgate)—Christ draws all of humanity and the whole of creation to himself.

While they rejoice during this present life in the gift of salvation, Christians look forward to the definitive realization of the Redemption in the age to come. After the trials and tribulations of history, all peoples "will see the Son of man coming in clouds with great power and glory" (Mk 13:26).

The Greek word for "coming," *parousia*, can also mean "presence." The word was used to indicate the solemn arrival of a ruler or a god. The majestic sense of this coming is also evident in the rest of the language which portrays this event. The description draws from the Old Testament expectation of the future age of the messiah.

The messianic time, as we have seen, has already been brought about through Christ's death and resurrection, and the descent of the Holy Spirit. Nonetheless, in the Second Coming the final transformation of humanity and all creation, begun in the resurrection of Christ, will reach its ultimate fulfillment.

With the *Parousia*, the history of salvation will arrive at its conclusion. The glorious Christ will judge the living and dead. The Lord's judgment on each person will not be simply a sentence pronounced from above. Rather, as the *Catechism of the Catholic Church* notes, "in the presence of Christ, who is Truth itself, the truth of each man's relationship with God will be laid bare" (1039). In the sight of the exalted Christ, the reality of each person's free response to God's grace or of the rejection of this grace will be made clear. The deeper divine meaning of all the events of history, so often hidden to our understanding here on earth, will become known.

In this climax of history, Christ will reveal the victory of God's justice over all the injustices committed by human beings. This day will be the true *Day of the Lord* foretold by the prophets, which will reveal the complete triumph of God and the destruction of evil (see Zep 2:3; Mal 4:1–5). God's glory will shine forth not simply in the resurrection of the just, but also in the divine judgment and punishment for sin. This judgment will wipe out the disorder caused by our injustices. But above all, the final judgment will be the moment for the supreme revelation of God's mercy and love. The infinite goodness of God will be perceptible precisely in the victory over evil.

Following the Last Judgment, those who have freely accepted the gift of redemption will be transformed according to the resurrection of Christ. Suffering will be no more, and God will bring each of us to the fullest realization of our being.

In the present life, Christians find true fulfillment in the sincere gift of ourselves in charity. In the life to come, this gift of self will be brought to a perfect actualization. Each redeemed person, fully transformed by the Holy Spirit in both body and soul, will live completely immersed in God's love. In and through this love, each person will exist in a communion of love with the rest of humanity. In a glorious manner, this communion will reflect and partake in the perfect communion of love found within the Holy Trinity.

This transformation, in the model of the risen Christ and in the power of the Holy Spirit, will affect not only persons but all of creation. The New Testament reminds us that Christians await, not simply the redemption of the body, but also a "new heavens and a new earth in which righteousness dwells" (2 Pt 3:13). The entire universe will experience a kind of death and rebirth similar to that which has occurred in Christ and which will occur in each redeemed person.

Only God's action will bring the world to this final radiant destiny. At the same time, the renewed cosmos will also bring completion to all of the efforts of men and women, throughout history, to build a more just and charitable world.

Regenerated through the definitive encounter with its glorious Lord, all of creation will be entirely filled with God's presence, without the mediation present in earthly life. As St. John states at the end of the Book of Revelation, "I saw no temple in the city, for its temple is the Lord God the Almighty and the Lamb" (Rv 21:22). The kingdom of God, which exists in a veiled and incomplete manner in history, will be wholly realized. Christ will reign forever, and in his lordship all things will fully exist for the glory of God (see 1 Cor 15:28).

This ultimate establishment of God's reign among us will not diminish, in any way, the value of created things. Rather, "the glory and the honor of the nations" will shine forth in the heavenly Jerusalem (Rv 21:26). All of creation, and the human person in particular, will reflect God's glory in a new and refulgent manner. Everything that is good, true, and beautiful in human life will take on an even greater splendor.

Strengthened by faith in Christ's saving death and resurrection, rejoicing in hope, and with the charity infused by the Holy Spirit, Christians eagerly look forward to this definitive liberation. They live with the certainty that God will fulfill the earnest desire for redemption, so deeply felt by men and women throughout history. God's gift of salvation will satisfy and perfect all of these longings in a renewed world in which God "will wipe away every tear from their eyes, and death shall be no more, neither shall there be mourning nor crying nor pain any more, for the former things have passed away" (Rv 21:4).

SOURCES

I have relied on various soteriology textbooks, in particular a recent one in Italian—Antonio Ducay, *Riportare il Mondo al Padre*—and also Fernando Ocáriz, Lucas F. Mateo-Seco, and Jose Antonio Riestra, *The Mystery of Jesus Christ*. The work of Michael Schmaus has also been invaluable, especially *Dogma*, volume 3, *God and His Christ*.

The use of these works and other textbooks has been supplemented with various scriptural commentaries, especially various essays from Gerhard Kittel and Gerhard Friedrich, eds., *Theological Dictionary of the New Testament*. Also indispensable has been the *Dictionary of Biblical Theology*, as well as the commentaries prepared by the Faculty of the University of Navarre in *The Navarre Bible*.

The documents of the Magisterium are always an important reference for soteriology. A key one for this work is Vatican II's Pastoral Constitution on the Church in the Modern World, *Gaudium et Spes*. The *Catechism of the Catholic Church*, a faithful summary of the Church's Tradition in light of Vatican II, has been a frequent reference point.

The International Theological Commission's document *Select Questions on the Theology of God the Redeemer*, from 1995, offers valuable insights into many of the key ideas in this book.

There have been a number of other important texts which deal with soteriological questions. Of course, there is Aquinas' *Summa Theologiae*. Other important works include Philippe de la Trinité's *What is Redemption?* and Romanus Cessario's more recent *The Godly Image: Christian Satisfaction in Aquinas*. Joseph Ratzinger's *Jesus of Nazareth* series, especially part two, *Holy Week: From the Entrance into Jerusalem to the Resurrection*, is filled with insights regarding soteriology. The same can be said, specifically with regard to the Fathers of the Church, for Brian E. Daley's recent study *God Visible: Patristic Christology Reconsidered*.

Abbreviations

CBD   Scott Hahn, ed. *Catholic Bible Dictionary*. New York: Doubleday, 2009.

CCC   *Catechism of the Catholic Church*. Washington, DC: Libreria Editrice Vaticana–United States Conference of Catholic Bishops, 1992.

CDF   Congregation for the Doctrine of the Faith

CE   Charles Herbermann et al. *The Catholic Encyclopedia*. 15 vols. New York: Encyclopedia Press, 1913. Online edition at New Advent. Ed. Kevin Knight. *https://www.newadvent.org/cathen/*.

CIPB   Josemaría Escrivá. *Christ is Passing By*. New York: Scepter Publishers, 1974. *https://www.escrivaworks.org/book/christ_is_passing_by-contents.htm*.

CMD   Manuel M. González Gil. *Cristo, El Misterio de Dios. Cristología y soteriología*. Madrid: Biblioteca de Autores Cristianos, 1976.

DBT   Xavier Leon-Dufour, ed. *Dictionary of Biblical Theology*. 2nd ed. Boston: St. Paul Books and Media, 1995.

GHC   Michael Schmaus. *Dogma*. Vol. 3, *God and his Christ*. Westminster, MD: Christian Classics, 1984.

GS   Paul VI. Constitution on the Church in the Modern World *Gaudium et Spes* (December 7, 1965). Vatican website: *www.vatican.va*.

GV   Brian E. Daley, SJ. *God Visible. Patristic Christology Reconsidered*. New York: Oxford University Press, 2019.

GWM   J.M. Casciaro and J.M. Monforte. *God, the World and Man in the Message of the Bible*. Translated by Michael Adams and James Gavigan. Dublin: Four Courts Press, 1996.

ITC   International Theological Commission. *Select Questions on the Theology of God the Redeemer*. (October 7, 1995). Vatican website: *http://www.vatican.va/roman_curia/congregations/cfaith/cti_documents/rc_cti_1995_teologia-redenzione_en.html*.

JBC   Raymond E. Brown, Joseph A. Fitzmyer, and Roland E. Murphy, eds. *The Jerome Biblical Commentary*, 2 vol. Englewood Cliff, NJ: Prentice Hall, 1968.

LG   Paul VI. Constitution on the Church Lumen Gentium (November 21, 1964). Vatican website: *www.vatican.va*.

MJC   Fernando Ocáriz, Lucas F. Mateo-Seco, and Jose Antonio Riestra. *The Mystery of Jesus Christ.* Translated by Michael Adams and James Gavigan. Portland, OR: Four Courts Press, 1994.

Nav-Pent   Faculty of Theology of the University of Navarre. *The Navarre Bible. The Pentateuch.* Translated by Michael Adams. Princeton, NJ: Scepter Publishers, 1999.

Nav-NT   Faculty of Theology of the University of Navarre. *The Navarre Bible. New Testament.* Translated by Michael Adams. New York: Scepter Publishers, 2008.

OIW   Athanasius. *On the Incarnation of the Word.* Translated by Archibald Robertson. In *Nicene and Post-Nicene Fathers, Second Series,* vol. 4. Edited by Philip Schaff and Henry Wace. Buffalo, NY: Christian Literature Publishing Co., 1892. Online edition at New Advent. Ed. Kevin Knight. *http://www.newadvent.org/fathers/2802.htm.*

OT   Old Testament

Ratzinger-Bap   Joseph Ratzinger. *Jesus of Nazareth: From the Baptism in the Jordan to the Transfiguration.* Translated by Adrian J. Walker. New York: Doubleday, 2007.

Ratzinger-HW   Joseph Ratzinger, *Jesus of Nazareth.* Part 2, *Holy Week: From the Entrance into Jerusalem to the Resurrection.* Translated by Philip J. Whitmore. San Francisco: Ignatius Press, 2011.

RH   John Paul II. Encyclical *Redemptor Hominis* (March 4, 1979). Vatican website: *www.vatican.va.*

RIM   Antonio Ducay. *Riportare il Mondo al Padre. Corso di Soteriologia Cristiana.* Rome: EDUSC, 2016.

Sal   Michael Patrick Barber. *Salvation. What Every Catholic Should Know.* San Francisco: Ignatius Press, 2019.

SC   José Antonio Sayés, *Señor y Cristo.* Pamplona, Spain: EUNSA, 1995.

ST   *The Summa Theologiae of St. Thomas Aquinas,* 2nd ed. Translated by Fathers of the English Dominican Province. 1920. Online edition at New Advent. Ed. Kevin Knight, 2017. *https://www.newadvent.org/summa/.*

TDNT   Gerhard Kittel and Gerhard Friedrich, eds. *Theological Dictionary of the New Testament.* Translated by and edited by Geoffrey W. Bromiley. 10 vols. Grand Rapids, MI: Wm. B. Eerdmans, 1967; reprinted 1995.

TSP Fernand Prat. *The Theology of Saint Paul.* Translated by John Stoddard. Vol. 1, from the eleventh French edition. Westminster, MD: The Newman Bookshop, 1926. Vol. 2, from the tenth French edition. Westminster, MD: The Newman Press, 1950.

WIR Philippe de la Trinité. *What is Redemption?* Translated by Anthony Armstrong. New York: Hawthorn Books, 1961.

Introduction

For background on Greek word *soter*, see Werner Foerster, "σωτήρ in the Greek World," in *TDNT*, vol. 7, 1004–1012. On the Church's insistence on the centrality of Christ, see for example, Pope Francis, Apostolic Exhortation *Evangelii Gaudium* (November 24, 2013), 11, Vatican website: *www.vatican. va*; see also Monsignor Fernando Ocáriz, *Pastoral Letter* (February 14, 2017), 8, *https://opusdei.org/en-us/document/letter-of-the-prelate-14-february-2017/*.

Chapter 1: Salvation: A Human Desire and Divine Gift

Opening quote: Jutta Burggraf, *Made for Freedom. Loving, Defending, and Living God's Gift* (New Rochelle, NY: Scepter, 2012), 22.

1A. Human Aspiration to Salvation, Constant in All History

"what divine revelation makes known . . .": *GS*, 13.

"Can't you see . . ." and "But of this . . .": Josemaría Escrivá, *Friends of God* (London: Scepter Publishers, 1981), 260, *https://www.escrivaworks. org/book/friends_of_god-chapter-16.htm*.

"For even in their misdeeds . . .": *OIW*, 3–4. Commentary on Eastern cultures (Confucius, Hinduism, Buddhism) as well as Greek culture based on Christopher Dawson, *Progress and Religion. An Historical Inquiry* (Washington, DC: The Catholic University of America Press, 1929), 98–104.

"By the fact of being . . .", "an "absolute reality": Burggraf, *Made for Freedom*, 24.

"Such a longing for salvation . . .": Commentary in this paragraph based on *RIM*, section 1.1. See also José Ignacio Murillo, *El Valor Revelador de la Muerte. Estudios desde Santo Tomás de Aquino* (Pamplona, Spain: Cuadernos de Anuario Filosófico Universidad de Navarra, 1999), 11–14.

"Along with death . . .": For discussion on evil here, see Alfred Sharpe, "Evil," in *CE*.

1B. Salvation, Initiative of the God of the Covenant

"in the face of . . .": *GS*, 10.

"it is this separation . . .": *CDF*, Letter On Certain Aspects of Christian Salvation *Placuit Deo* (January 24, 2018), 7, Vatican website: *www.vatican.va*. The text makes reference to Rom 5:12.

"the Church firmly believes . . .": *GS*, 10.

With regard to salvation defined in terms of God's will to enter into dialogue with man, see Michael Schmaus, *Dogma 1: God in Revelation* (London: Sheed and Ward, 1968), 140.

On covenant, see *GWM*, 316. Regarding analysis of Hebrew *yasha*, see *GWM*, 390.

"fundamental experience . . ."; "to be saved . . .": Colomban Lesquivit and Pierre Grelot, "Salvation," trans. Eugene C. Ulrich, in *DBT*, 518–519; analysis of the Old Testament (hereafter "OT") concept of salvation, and the correlation between salvation and judgment, draw from the same source. For analysis of OT concept of kingdom, see *GWM*, 381, 386, 390–391.

1C. Christ, Universal Savior

On the law as manifesting sin, see *Nav-NT*, commentary on Rom 7:7–13.

"Still, the New Testament makes it clear . . .": Some examples are Lk 7:48 and Jn 8:34. See Lesquivit and Grelot, "Salvation," in *DBT*, 521.

"marked by a strong . . .": *CDF*, *Placuit Deo*, 2. For commentary on subjectivist vision of salvation, see 2–3 of this document. Commentary on the effect of salvation on the entire human condition and creation draws from the same text.

"The early Church sought . . .": paragraph draws from *GV*, 61 (regarding St. Justin), 71 (on material aspect of liberation), 93 (on Christ as true knowledge).

On the relationship between salvation and peace, see *GHC*, 82.

With regard to peace as a right ordering, and peace in relationship with justice, see *GS*, 78.

On the perspectives which negate the exclusive meaning of Christ's salvific action, see *CDF*, Declaration On the Unicity and Salvific Universality of Jesus Christ and the Church *Dominus Iesus* (August 6, 2000), 9, Vatican website: *www.vatican.va*.

Apropos of the Church's "essential visible aspect" and invisible mystery, see *LG*, 5.

"In the New Testament, the mystery of Jesus . . .": *CDF*, *Dominus Iesus*, 12. Commentary in this paragraph is based on this text. Quoted passage makes reference to Acts 2:32–36; Jn 7:39, 20:22; 1 Cor 15:45 (on effusion of Holy Spirit in "messianic times") and 1 Cor 10:4; 1 Pt 1:10–12 (on effusion of Holy Spirit prior to Christ's "coming in history").

With respect to the "invisible and mysterious ways" of the Spirit, see *GS*, 22.

"Jesus Christ has a significance . . .": *CDF, Dominus Iesus*, 15.

Chapter 2: The Concept of Redemption

2A. The Meaning of Redemption

On distinction between redemption and salvation, see *Sal*, 38. With regard to original Greek sense of "redemption" and OT notion of redemption, see *GWM*, 391–392.

Regarding Levirate marriage, see *Nav-Pent*, commentary on Dt 25:5–19.

On OT notion of redemption and ransom, see *Nav-Pent*, commentary on Lv 25:23.

On sense of redemption by a family member, see *Sal*, 39. Definition of *padah*: see *GWM*, 392.

With regard to characteristics of ransom in Jewish Law, see David P. Moessner, "Redemption," in *The Oxford Encyclopedia of the Bible and Theology*, online edition, ed. Samuel E. Balentine (Oxford University Press, 2014), *http://dx.doi.org/10.1093/acref:obso/9780199858699.001.0001*.

"According to Jewish interpreters, this blood . . .": see *Sal*, 43–44.

See also this text with regard to Moses' petition for atonement. "the word 'atonement' (Hebrew *kipper*) . . ."; "'atonement' refers to delivering . . .": *Sal*, 45.

With regard to the covenant at Sinai as a continuation of the covenant made at creation, see Scott Hahn, *A Father Who Keeps His Promises: God's Covenant Love in Scripture* (Ann Arbor, MI: Servant Publications, 1998), 35, 47–48.

See this same work, 74–75, on how sin and death offer an opportunity for man's self-gift in love.

2B. Errors on the Nature of Redemption

"no doubt many . . .": *GS*, 10.

The subsequent quotations draw from the same text: "Thinking they have found . . ." and "strive to confer . . ." The description of self-redemption in Gnosticism draws from Paul O'Callaghan, *Children of God in the World: An Introduction to Theological Anthropology* (Washington, DC: The Catholic University of America Press, 2016), 143.

On Pelagius' vision of self-redemption by man's own effort, see Ludwig Ott, *Fundamentals of Catholic Dogma*, trans. Patrick Lynch, 4th ed. (Rockford, IL: Tan Books, 1960), 178.

For commentary on Pelagius' theory of redemption, see O'Callaghan, *Children of God in the World*, 159–160; see the same work, 173, on the other extreme of double predestination.

"there has never been . . .": quoted in O'Callaghan, *Children of God in the World*, 173.

Apropos "the great diversity of perspectives" on redemption, see *ITC*, I.30.

2C. Non-Christian Conceptions of Redemption

On redemption in the various world religions, see *ITC*: with regard to Hinduism, I.18–19; on Buddhism, I.22; on Islam, I.25.

On redemption in the traditional and tribal religions, see I.28.

2D. Redemption and Salvation: Necessity of Redemption for the Salvation of Man

Aquinas on the need for one who is both God and man to make proper atonement: see *ST*, III, q. 1, art. 2, ad. 2.

On the necessity for God to redeem us, see St. Anselm of Canterbury, *Cur Deus homo* II, 4, in *Works of St. Anslem*, trans. Sidney Norton Deane (London: Methuen, 1903), online edition at Internet Sacred Texts Archive, Evinity Publishing, *https://www.sacred-texts.com/chr/ans/ans117.htm*.

"the necessity for God to be both 'victim' and 'hero' . . .": David P. Moessner, "Redemption."

On God saving us without intermediaries, and becoming one of us, see *ITC*, IV.20. "the God of creation is revealed . . .": *RH*, 9. The final sentence follows 10 of the same document.

Chapter 3: The Mediation of Christ

Opening quote: *CDF, Dominus Iesus*, 11. The Congregation cites *GS*, 45. It also makes reference to the Council of Trent, *Decree on Original Sin* (June 17, 1546), 3.

3A. The Concept of Mediation

On concept of mediation in the Hellenic world, see A. Oepke, "μεσίτης, μεσιτεηύω," in *TDNT*, vol. 4, 599.

"At first glance, this word . . .": for commentary on God's immediacy to man in this paragraph, see *MJC*, 139.

"you were more inward . . .": Augustine, *Confessions*, trans. J.G. Pilkington, in *Nicene and Post-Nicene Fathers*, 1st ser., vol. 1., ed. Philip Schaff (Buffalo, NY: Christian Literature Publishing Co., 1887), online ed. at New Advent, ed. Kevin Knight, bk. 3, chaps. 6, 11, *http://www.newadvent.org/fathers/110103.htm*.

On the beatific vision as "immediate perception of God's glory," see *CCC*, 1028.

"an ineffable mystery"; "Even when he does . . .": Schmaus, *God in Revelation*, 42.

Regarding sin as real separation between man and God, see *MJC*, 139–140.

On the Law and worship as sources of mediation between God and Chosen People, see *RIM*, 78.

On persons as mediators in the OT, see the same work, 78; on Moses, see footnote in *RIM*, 78.

Regarding the Servant of Yahweh: the poems on this theme are Is 42:1–7, Is 49:1–9, Is 50:4–9, and Is 52:13–53:12. For an overview of this theme, see *MJC*, 37.

On the lack of a Hebrew equivalent for "mediator" and the belief in mediators in the ancient world, see André-Alphonse Viard and Jean Duplacy, "Mediator," trans. William J. Young, in *DBT*, 344.

On the distinctiveness of the OT idea of mediation, in contrast with the pagan view, see Oepke, "μεσίτης, μεσιτεηύω," 604–608.

In reference to the Law of Israel's recognition of mediation, as involving two parties of equal standing, see Viard and Duplacy, "Mediator," 344.

On presence of *munus triplex* "within and outside the Bible," see Oepke, "μεσίτης, μεσιτεηύω," 604–608.

3B. Existence and Nature of the Mediation of Christ

On non-use of "mediator" in the Gospels, see Oepke, "μεσίτης, μεσιτεηύω," in *TDNT*, vol. 4, 618.

On the significance of the mountain in ancient times and in Scripture, see Xavier Léon-Dufour, "Mountain," trans. Thomas M. Spittler, in *DBT*, 372.

Regarding Christ's ascent to the mountain for the Beatitudes, and the descent to the plain, see *Ratzinger-Bap*, 66–69.

Commentary on Mt 11:27 draws from *SC*, 203.

On the unique role of Christ's mediation, presented by St. John, see Oepke, "μεσίτης, μεσιτεηύω," 623–624.

On the "ancient pagan view" of mediators and on Christ as fulfilling the mediation present in the Suffering Servant, see the same work, 621–623.

For commentary on St. Paul's view of mediation and also concluding observation on Christ's salvific mediation, in contrast with Greek cosmic mediation, see Oepke, "μεσίτης, μεσιτεηύω," 622–623.

"By his entire life . . .": see Paul VI, Constitution on Divine Revelation *Dei Verbum* (November 18, 1965), 4, Vatican website: *www.vatican.va.*

3C. Mediation and Hypostatic Union

Regarding commentary on Gal 3:19: There are different interpretations of this Scripture verse, but the general sense of the text conveys a connection between mediation and the imperfect nature of the Law. See Oepke, "μεσίτης, μεσιτεηύω," 619.

"which took place . . .": Leo the Great, *Letter 28*, 'The Tome', trans. Charles Lett Feltoe, in *Nicene and Post-Nicene Fathers*, 2nd ser., vol. 12, ed. Philip Schaff and Henry Wace (Buffalo, NY: Christian Literature Publishing Co., 1895), online ed. at New Advent, ed. Kevin Knight, 2, *http://www.newadvent.org/fathers/3604028.htm.*

On one who is fully man and fully God making atonement, see Ott, *Fundamentals of Catholic Dogma*, 179.

On Christ's role as "head of mankind" and "natural representative of the human race" through the hypostatic union, see Joseph Wilhelm, "Mediator (Christ as Mediator)," in *CE*.

On intercession, see "huperentugchanó," in *Strong's Concordance* (Bible Hub), *https://biblehub.com/greek/5241.htm.*

"a contracted obligation . . .": Oepke, "μεσίτης, μεσιτεηύω," 620.

On the significance of the curtain, see *Nav-NT*, commentary to Heb 10:19–39 and "Veil" in *CBD*, 938;

with regard to the connection with Mark 15:38, see Myles M. Bourke, "The Epistle to the Hebrews," in *JBC*, vol. 2, 400.

3D. Mediator and Mediators

"one Mediator," "established and continually sustains," "communicated truth and grace to all": *LG*, 8.

"the invisible God (see Col 1:15, 1 Tm 1:17) out of the abundance of His love speaks to men as friends (see Ex 33:11; Jn 15:14–15) and lives among them (see Bar 3:38) . . .": Paul VI, *Dei Verbum*, 2.

"in no wise obscures . . .": *LG*, 60. "an apostle—that is what . . ."; "Each of us . . .": *CIPB*, 120.

Chapter 4: The Three Offices of Christ

Opening quote: St. John Henry Newman, "Sermon 5.

The Three Offices of Christ," in *Sermons on Subjects of the Day* (1843), new impression, New York: Longmans, Green, and Co., 1902; online edition at *Newman Reader*, The National Institute for Newman Studies, 2007, *https://www.newmanreader.org/works/subjects/sermon5.html.*

On Jesus uniting and fulfilling the three roles of mediation, see Augustin George, "Priesthood," trans. Eugene C. Ulrich, in *DBT*, 463.

With regard to the importance of these roles starting with Moses, see *RIM*, 78.

"king, the prophet, and the priest are not significant for what they are . . .": see *RIM*, 80.

4A. The Royal or Pastoral Ministry of Christ

On Revelation as purifying the idea of kingship, see Gerhard von Rad, "B. הֶלֶם and תּוּכְלָם in the OT," in *TDNT*, 1, 566.

Regarding God as initially fulfilling the role of king in Israel, see Pierre Grelot, "King," trans. Eugene C. Ulrich, in *DBT*, 288.

"Royalty was associated with God . . .": see *RIM*, 82. "The later history of Israel . . ." see Grelot, "King," 289.

On the organizational unity of a king desired by Israel, see *RIM*, 79.

Concerning the significance of anointing kings with oil, see Louis Isaac Rabinowitz, "Anointing," in *Encyclopedia Judaica* (The Gale Group, 2008), online edition at Jewish Virtual Library, *https://www.jewishvirtuallibrary. org/anointing.*

"During the time of King David": see Grelot, "King," 288. On prophecy of the end of kingship, see the same work, 89.

On kingship becoming more eternal and universal, see von Rad, "B. הֶלֶם and תּוּכְלָם in the OT," 570–571.

In reference to the "strong political aspect" of messianic expectation, see Grelot, "King," 290.

On early Christians' hesitancy to use title of king for Jesus, see Karl Ludwig Schmidt, "E. The Word Group βασιλεύς κτλ. in the NT," in *TDNT*, vol. 1, 578.

"It is a spiritual kingdom . . .": see Grelot, "King," 291.

"is the salvation of the individual . . .": Pius XI, Encyclical Letter On the Feast of Christ the King *Quas Primas* (December 11, 1925), 18, Vatican website: *www.vatican.va.*

On kingship founded on the hypostatic union, see the same encyclical, 13.

Regarding Christ's role as lawgiver and judge, see *MJC*, 143.

On Christ's humanity as showing "the true significance of God's kingdom," see *RIM*, 88. "Truth and justice . . .": *CIPB*, 180.

4B. The Prophetic Ministry of Christ

On role of oracles in ancient times, see Paul Beauchamp, "Prophet," trans. Joseph A. Bracken, in *DBT*, 468.

"declaring, proclaiming . . .": Helmut Krämer, "προφήτης κτλ. A. The Word Group in Profane Greek," in *TDNT*, vol. 6, 795.

Regarding the Hebrew sense of the word prophet, see Rudolf Meyer, "προφήτης κτλ. B.אִבָא in the Old Testament," in *TDNT*, vol. 6, 796.

On a prophet as one who passes on a "living and vital force," see O. Procksch, "λέγω. C. The Word of God in the Old Testament," in *TDNT*, vol. 4, 95.

With regard to "similar gestures" found in other prophets, see Faculty of Theology of the University of Navarre, *The Navarre Bible: Major Prophets*, trans. Michael Adams (New York: Scepter, 2005), commentary on Jer 1:4–10.

On the role of prophet in contrast with king and priest, see *RIM*, 79.

On the sense of prophet as teller of future, brought about through Christianity, see Krämer, "προφήτης," *TDNT*, vol. 6, 795.

"Their message has relevance . . .": see Beauchamp, "Prophet," 471–472.

Regarding the early Church's reluctance to use title "prophet" with regard to Jesus, see Gerhard Friedrich, "προφήτης κτλ. D. Prophets and Prophecies in the New Testament," in *TDNT*, vol. 6, 848.

"the full revelation . . .": Paul VI, *Dei Verbum*, 7. The text makes reference to 2 Cor 1:20, 3:13, 4:6.

"Going far beyond these prophets": see *MJC*, 147.

4C. The Priestly Mediation of Jesus Christ

On priesthood in ancient times, see Gottlob Shrenk, "ἱερός," in *TDNT*, vol. 3, 257–258, 260.

On the special mission of priests in the Old Covenant, see *RIM*, 93–94.

On the inefficacy of OT sacrifices for taking away sin, see Heb 5:2; see also Gottlob Shrenk "ἀρχιερεύς," in *TDNT*, vol. 3, 277–278.

With regard to the condemnation of the sons of Eli, see Faculty of Theology of the University of Navarre, *The Navarre Bible: Joshua—Kings*, trans. Michael Adams (Princeton, NJ: Scepter, 2002), commentary on 1 Sm 2:27–36.

For Augustine's commentary on the change of priesthood, see Augustine, *City of God*, trans. Marcus Dods, in *Nicene and Post-Nicene Fathers*, 1st ser., vol. 2, ed. Philip Schaff (Buffalo, NY: Christian Literature Publishing Co., 1887), online ed. at New Advent, ed. Kevin Knight, bk. 17, chaps. 5–6, *http://www.newadvent.org/fathers/120117.htm*.

On Melchizedek as "apt figure" for eternal priesthood, see note to Hebrews 7:1–3, in *The New American Bible, Revised Edition* (Washington, DC: United States Conference of Catholic Bishops, 2011), *http://www.usccb.org/bible/*.

Regarding the distinctiveness of eternal priesthood, see Shrenk, "ἀρχιερεύς," 275.

On Christ as possessing an eternal priesthood through the hypostatic union, see Hebrews 2:10–18; 5:7ff; see George, "Priesthood," in *DBT*, 463.

The most common opinion is that Christ's priesthood is constituted by the hypostatic union itself. Regarding different views on this question, see *MJC*, 173–175.

On Christ's identity as Son giving a new dynamism to the role of priest, see Shrenk, "ἀρχιερεύς," 276.

Regarding replacement of sacrifice of animal flesh with the action of the Spirit, see Shrenk, "ἀρχιερεύς," 280–281.

Chapter 5: The Mysteries of the Life of Christ and their Redemptive Efficacy

Opening quote: from St. Teresa of Avila, "To the Birth of Jesus," in *The Collected Works of St. Teresa of Avila*, vol. 3, trans. Kieran Kavanaugh and Otilio Rodriguez (Washington, DC: ICS Publications, 1985), 387.

5A. The Redemptive Meaning Present in All of Christ's Life

"it is his very *person* itself": *GV*, 279.

On God changing "the course of human nature" by the Incarnation: see, for example, Augustine's vision of the Incarnation, described in *GV*, 170–171.

Regarding Christ's glory which is fully achieved with the Resurrection, and which points to the glory which is hidden and in potential in Christ's earthly life: see *CCC*, 645–646.

5B. The Infancy and Hidden Life of Jesus

Christ "was made man that we might be made God": *OIW*, 54. "fully reveals man . . .": *GS*, 22.

On Incarnation as action of the Holy Spirit and analysis of Lk 1:35, see *SC*, 55–56.

Regarding Mary as "new tabernacle": Cándido Pozo, *María en la Escritura y en la Fe de la Iglesia* (Madrid: BAC popular, 1979), 78, cited in *SC*, 56.

Concerning the essence of the Redemption as Christ's offering of himself in love, see *MJC*, 200.

On the universal significance of the Epiphany, see *CCC*, 528.

"the inner aspiration": Joseph Ratzinger, *Jesus of Nazareth: The Infancy Narratives* (New York: Image, 2012), 97; see the same work, 95–96, for commentary on the Epiphany as fulfilling human knowledge.

With regard to the significance of Jesus's circumcision and presentation, see *RIM*, 128–129.

On Jesus' submission to the Law, see *RIM*, 130.

On the meaning of Jesus' Hebrew name, see commentary on Mt 1, 18–25, in *Nav-NT*.

Regarding the meaning of Jesus' childhood, see *CCC*, 526.

On Jesus' circumcision as foreshadowing baptism, see *CCC*, 527.

"the fact that . . ."; "the carpenter . . ."; "he was God . . .": *CIPB*, 14.

On Jesus' hidden life as "undoing the disobedience of Adam," see *CCC*, 532.

5C. The Public Life of Jesus

On the overall significance of the public ministry, see *RIM*, 132. With regard to true "baptism" as Christ's own passion, see *CCC*, 536.

On the meaning of immersion in water in the ancient mindset, see *Ratzinger-Bap*, 15. "his inaugural gesture . . .": *Ratzinger-Bap*, 18.

Concerning the Church Fathers' view of Christ's baptism, see again the same work, 25.

"to purify the waters": Ambrose, *Commentary on Luke*, 3:21–24 (Patristic Bible Commentary), *https://sites.google.com/site/aquinasstudybible/home/luke-commentary/ambrose-of-milan-commentary-on-luke*.

On the Christian's sharing in the priestly, prophetic, and kingly identity of Christ, see *LG*, 31.

With regard to Christ's victory over temptations as a victory over the threefold attraction of sin, see *Sal*, 172–174.

This work makes reference to John Bergsma and Brant Pitre, *A Catholic Introduction to the Bible: The Old Testament* (San Francisco: Ignatius Press, 2018), 126–127.

On St. Luke's telling of the devil's return at Christ's passion, see Ducay, *RIM*, 138. Regarding the temptation to seek a "worldly political kingdom," see *Ratzinger-Bap*, 39–40.

On Mt 27:38–40 as a summary of the temptations of Christ, see *RIM*, 138.

Concerning Jesus' preaching as a radical step forward in closeness to the Father, see Lucas F. Mateo-Seco, *Dios Uno y Trino* (Pamplona, Spain: EUNSA, 2008), 110–111.

On this closeness of God as revealing arrival of kingdom of God, see *SC*, 77.

With regard to the original sense of the words for "miracle," see George Bertram, "θαῦμα," in *TDNT*, vol. 3, 29.

On the wonder which does not lead to faith, as in Lk 7:9, see same entry in *TDNT*, 40.

Apropos of the connections between the OT and the Transfiguration, see Paul de Surgy, "Transfiguration," trans. Donald F. Brezine, in *DBT*, 611.

See *ST*, III, q. 45, art. 4, ad. 2 for Aquinas' description of the Transfiguration as prefiguring the resurrection of the elect.

On the miraculous change of form after the resurrection in late Jewish thought, see J. Behm, "μεταμορφόω," in *TDNT*, vol. 3, 757.

In reference to the Transfiguration as preparing the apostles for the message of suffering, see *Ratzinger-Bap*, 311–313. From this same work, 311, is: "a glory, however . . ."

Chapter 6: The Sacrifice of the Cross

Opening quote: From Office of Readings for Memorial of Saint Teresa Benedicta of the Cross, *Edith Stein Werke* (Freiburg, 1987), 11:124–126.

6A. The Predictions of Christ regarding his Death: The Last Supper and the Meaning of the Passion

On Jesus' awareness of his future suffering, as seen in Mk 6:5, see *SC*, 220. With reference to Christ's immediate knowledge of the Father, see *MJC*, 152–154.

On the redemptive meaning of Christ's predictions of his death, see *CMD*, 26.

Regarding Christ's awareness of the meaning of his death at the Last Supper, see *MJC*, 209–210.

On the true worship inaugurated in Christ's blood, see *Ratzinger-HW*, 134. See the same work, 112–113, on likely date of the Crucifixion as the day before Passover.

On the washing of the feet and man's need to be served by Christ, see *CMD*, 24–25.

6B. The Circumstances of the Passion of Christ

On the perceived threat posed by Jesus to "fundamental principles" of the Chosen People, see *CCC*, 576, 587, 589.

With regard to the roots of Jesus' condemnation in an unwillingness to change outlook, see *CCC*, 591.

For commentary on the raising of Lazarus, see Bruce Vawter, "The Gospel According to John," in *JBC*, vol. 2, 446.

"only through the total loss": *Ratzinger-HW*, 171.

Regarding commentary on Caiaphas' prediction, see the same source, 171, 174.

In reference to the original Jewish hope of Caiaphas' words: The same source, 171, cites Charles K. Barrett, *The Gospel according to St. John*, 2nd ed. (London: SPCK, 1978), 407.

On the nature of the Sanhedrin, see Edward J. Mally, "The Gospel According to Mark," in *JBC*, vol. 2, 56.

Concerning the first stage of trial as cross-examination, see *Ratzinger-HW*, 175–176.

Commentary on the nature of Christ's blasphemy as being equal to God draws from Mally, "The Gospel According to Mark," 56.

Regarding the claim to messiahship as not in itself an offense, see John L. McKenzie, "The Gospel According to Matthew," in *JBC*, vol. 2, 110.

On the political dimension which Christ's accusers emphasize before Pilate, see *Ratzinger-HW*, 183.

Regarding the charge of claiming to be king, see McKenzie, "The Gospel According to Matthew," 111; see also *Ratzinger-HW*, 189.

"Such tactics were common": see Vawter, "The Gospel According to John," 460.

On the crowd as being deceived by an "earthly and political" vision of the messiah, see *CMD*, 34.

In reference to crucifixion as common capital punishment, see Josephus, *Life* 75, 420, and *Jewish War*, 2.14, 9, 306; cited in Mally, "The Gospel According to Mark," 57.

6C. The Causes of the Passion and Death of Christ

On Judas' initiative in Christ's passion, see McKenzie, "The Gospel According to Matthew," in *JBC*, vol. 2, 108.

"In her Magisterial teaching . . .": *CCC*, 598; words from *Roman Catechism*, cited here, are from I, 5, 11; the footnote in the *CCC* makes reference to Heb 12:3.

"are no more . . .": *CMD*, 37.

See the same source, 42, with regard to "what God the Father has fundamentally willed."

6D. The Initiative of the Father and the "Abandonment" of Jesus

On the Father willing Christ's death to accomplish the Redemption and manifest God's love, see *CMD*, 45; see also *ITC*, IV.36.

Regarding the will of the Father as command, see *MJC*, 211.

On the interpretation of Christ's final words as an "abandonment" by the Father, see *MJC*, 215. "Jesus is praying": *Ratzinger-HW*, 214.

6E. The Glory of the Cross

On Jesus taking on the greatest of suffering and transforming it, see *Ratzinger-HW*, 214.

In reference to the double meaning of being "lifted up" in St. John, see Vawter, "The Gospel According to John," in *DBC*, vol. 2, 430.

Regarding the reality of Christ's dead body and concurrent identity as God, see Lucas F. Mateo-Seco, "Muerte de Cristo y teología de la cruz. Reflexiones sobre la metodologia cristológica," in *Cristo, Hijo de Dios y Redentor del Hombre: III Simposio Internacional de Teología de la Universidad de Navarra*, ed. Lucas F. Mateo Seco et al. (Navarre, Spain: Servicio de Publicaciones de la Universidad de Navarra, 1982), 706, *https://dadun.unav.edu/handle/10171/6402*.

On the Cross as revealing God's holiness in a maximum way, see *CMD*, 59.

With regard to Cross as the supreme act of worship, see *Ratzinger-HW*, 223.

Chapter 7: The Redemptive Value of the Sacrifice of Christ (I)

Opening quote: from Jutta Burggraf, "Christian Mortification—Praying in Body and Soul," Opus Dei website, 2020, *https://opusdei.org/en/article/praying-body-and-soul/*.

7A. The Merit of the Sufferings and Death of Christ

"merited Justification for us": Council of Trent, *Decree on Justification* (January 13, 1547), chap. 7, *http://www.thecounciloftrent.com/ch6.htm*.

On the existence of moral order with reward and punishment, see *MJC*, 288.
For the commentary on Phil 2:8–9, see *MJC*, 288–289.
Regarding congruous merit, see Joseph Pohle, "Merit," in *CE*.

7B. The Notion of Satisfaction

On the distinction between guilt and punishment, see Romanus Cessario, *The Godly Image: Christian Satisfaction in Aquinas* (Washington, DC: The Catholic University of America Press, 2020), 109.

"He who does not render": Anselm of Canterbury, *Cur Deus Homo*, bk. 1, chap. 11, *https://www.sacred-texts.com/chr/ans/ans117.htm*.

"so long as he does not restore": same work, bk. 1, chap. 11. On the root of the word "satisfaction," see *The Concise Oxford Dictionary of English Etymology*, ed. T.F. Hoad, online ed. (Oxford University Press, 2003), s.v. "satisfaction," *https://www.oxfordreference.com/view/10.1093acref/9780192830 982.001.0001/acref-9780192830982*.

On sin as disturbance of right order, see Cessario, *Godly Image*, 7, 111–113, 245.

In reference to the search for a substitute for punishment in non-Christian religions, see *Ratzinger-HW*, 172–173.

Regarding transfer of sins in OT sacrifices through laying of hands, see *Nav-Pent*, commentary on Lv 1:4.

On Moses' offering of himself for the peoples' sins, see *Ratzinger-HW*, 173.

On Anselm's position that a God-man must make satisfaction, see his *Cur Deus Homo*, bk. 2, chap. 6.

Aquinas quotes the words from St. John's Gospel in *ST*, q. 46, art. 1. Text of St. John's Gospel is taken from this text of *ST*.

7C. The Passion and Death of Christ as Satisfaction

"Christ's gratuitous offering . . ." see *RIM*, 56.

On St. Peter's words connecting Christ with the Suffering Servant, see *MJC*, 272.

With regard to the opposition between "one" and "all" in the description of the New Adam, see L. Cerfaux, *Christ in the Theology of St. Paul*, trans. Geoffrey Webb and Adrian Walker (New York, NY: Herder and Herder, 1959), 231.

On Adam as type for Christ, see "Strong's NT 5179: τύπος," in *Thayer's Greek Lexicon* (Biblesoft, 2011; at Bible Hub), *https://biblehub.com/greek/5179.htm*.

For St. Irenaeus of Lyons' teaching on the Incarnation as leading man to God, and "redeeming us by His own blood": Irenaeus of Lyons, *Against Heresies*, trans. Alexander Roberts and William Rambaut, in *Ante-Nicene Fathers*, vol. 1, eds. Alexander Roberts, James Donaldson, and A. Cleveland Coxe (Buffalo, NY: Christian Literature Publishing Co., 1885), online edition New Advent, ed. Kevin Knight, bk. 5, chap. 1, *https://www.newadvent. org/fathers/0103501.htm*.

On Irenaeus' position with regard to the reasonableness of the Redemption, see *ITC*, III.5.

"giving His soul for our souls": Irenaeus of Lyons, *Against Heresies*, bk. 5, chap. 1.

On the Fathers' recognition of sin as loss of order in the "whole of being," see *GHC*, 86.

"Christ has assumed a human nature . . .": see Athanasius, *Discourse 2 Against the Arians*, trans. John Henry Newman and Archibald Robertson, in *Nicene and Post-Nicene Fathers*, 2nd ser., vol. 4, eds. Philip Schaff and Henry Wace (Buffalo, NY: Christian Literature Publishing Co., 1892). online ed. at New Advent, ed. Kevin Knight, 68–69, *http://www.newadvent.org/ fathers/28162.htm*; see also commentary in *ITC*, III, 7.

The diminished state of human nature assumed by Christ would include the capacity to suffer and die; see *MJC*, 61.

"The Humanity of God": Gregory of Nanzianzus, *Orations*, trans. Charles Gordon Browne and James Edward Swallow, in *Nicene and Post-Nicene Fathers*, 2nd ser., vol. 7., eds. Philip Schaff and Henry Wace (Buffalo, NY: Christian Literature Publishing Co., 1894), online ed. at New Advent, ed. Kevin Knight, 45.22, *http://www.newadvent.org/fathers/310245.htm*; see ITC, III, 8.

On the sense given by Tertullian to satisfaction, see Robert D. Culver, "The Doctrine Of Atonement Before Anselm," in *Global Journal of Classic Theology* 4, no. 3 (October 2004), *https://www.globaljournalct.com/ the-doctrine-of-atonement-before-anselm/*.

"penal function": Hilary of Poitiers, *Homilies on the Psalms*, trans. E.W. Watson and L. Pullan, in *Nicene and Post-Nicene Fathers*, 2nd ser., vol. 9, eds. Philip Schaff and Henry Wace. (Buffalo, NY: Christian Literature Publishing Co., 1899), online ed. at New Advent, ed. Kevin Knight, Ps 53, 12–13, *http://www.newadvent.org/fathers/3303.htm*.

On the development of the legal approach to sin in Roman and Germanic culture, see *GHC*, 86.

Regarding Anselm's emphasis on God's fulfillment of the "the strictest requirements of justice," see *MJC*, 277.

On Aquinas' going beyond earlier explanations of satisfaction, see Cessario, *Godly Image*, 241–242.

Commentary on personalist aspect of Aquinas' teaching is based on the same source, 145–152.

"By suffering out of love and obedience . . .": *ST*, III, q. 48, art. 2, "*On the contrary* . . ." "the dignity of His life" and for commentary on Christ's satisfaction as belonging to all the faithful: *ST*, III, q. 48, art. 2, ad. 1.

On Christ's suffering as the "very greatest of pain," see *ST*, III, q. 46, art. 6. For reference to Christ's suffering in light of Mt 5:10, see *ST*, III, q. 48, art. 1, "*On the contrary* . . ." "offers something which the offended one loves": *ST*, III, q. 48, art. 2, "*On the contrary*." On the pain of Christ as atoning for man's excessive self-satisfaction, see *WIR*, 76. "it is just": *ST*, III, q. 86, art. 4, "*I answer that*."

"is capable of doing," and also with regard to Christ's suffering as the manifestation of God's love: Jutta Burggraf, "Christian Mortification—Praying in Body and Soul," Opus Dei website, 2020, *https://opusdei.org/en/article/praying-body-and-soul/*.

"a complete submission": Cessario, *Godly Image*, 245.

See the same source, 245, on Christ's justice as restoring man's communion with the Trinity. "superabundance of love": John Paul II, *Audience* (October 26, 1988). Translation from Italian is ours.

Regarding how any act of charity and obedience of Christ makes satisfaction, see *MJC*, 286.

"in Jesus a power . . .": *GHC*, 87.

On Protestant Reformers' view of penal substitution, see *WIR*, 16, 21. On Christ making expiation by his suffering, see *MJC*, 275. Regarding love as the difference between punishment and satisfaction, see *WIR*, 75.

On charity as necessary for satisfaction in Aquinas' view, see *ST*, *Supplement to the Third Part*, q. 14, art. 2. "merited Justification for us": Council of Trent, *Decree on Justification*, chap. 7.

Chapter 8: The Redemptive Value of the Sacrifice of Christ (II)

Opening quote: from Office of Readings for Memorial of St. Bridget of Sweden. From the prayers attributed to St. Bridget of Sweden, *Revelationum S. Brigittae*, bk. 2 (Rome, 1628), 408–410.

8A. Sacrifice in the Old Testament

On the etymological significance of sacrifice, see "sacrifice," in *The Oxford Companion to Classical Literature*, M. C. Howatson, ed., online ed. (Oxford University Press, 2011), 1, *https://doi.org/10.1093/acref/9780199548545.001.0001*.

On the most important sacrifices being animal sacrifices, see *The Oxford Classical Dictionary*, ed. Simon Hornblower and Antony Spawforth, online ed., s.v. "animals in cult," *https://doi.org/10.1093/acref/9780198606413.001.0001*.

Concerning the distinction of Jewish sacrifices from pagan ones, see Johannes Behm, "θύω," in *TDNT*, vol. 3, 183.

"Pagan sacrifices, on the other hand": see Howatson, "sacrifice."

On the concrete places associated with God in OT sacrifice, see "Tabernacle," in *CBD*, 884.

"burnt in its entirety": *Nav-Pent*, footnote to Lv 1:1–17. Subsequent description of holocaust and the other types of sacrifices draws from the commentary on the respective verses of Leviticus.

On blood as source of life and symbol of God, see "Blood" in *CBD*, 123.

With regard to the particular role of shedding of blood in the OT, see *WIR*, 137. "it was common to offer God the first yield": see Charles Souvay, "Offerings," in *CE*.

On frankincense, see Roland J. Faley, "Leviticus," in *JBC*, vol. 1, 69. See the same reference on "sharing" of food in peace offerings. "disturbed the right order of things": same work, 70.

With regard to going "outside the camp," see Helmet Koester, "Outside the Camp: Hebrews 13.9–14," in *Harvard Theological Review* 55, no. 4 (1962): 301.

For a description of animal sacrifice outside the tabernacle or at the Holy of Holies, see Faley, "Leviticus," 70.

8B. The Sacrifices of the Old Testament Fulfilled in Christ

Commentary on sacrifice draws from *RIM*, 95, 165–167.

On the inefficacy of OT sacrifices for taking away sin, see Gottlob Shrenk "ἀρχιερεύς," in *TDNT*, vol. 3, 277–278.

Regarding this same topic see Hermann Schultz, "The Significance of Sacrifice in the Old Testament," *American Journal of Theology* 4, no. 2 (1900): 264–265, *http://www.jstor.org/stable/3153112*.

On the relationship between OT sacrifices and sin, see also David Montgomery, "Forgiveness 2. Forgiveness in the Old Testament," ed. Stephen Graham, in *Embodying Forgiveness* Project (Centre for Contemporary Christianity in Ireland), 3, *http://www.contemporarychristianity.net/resources/pdfs/Forgiveness_Paper_02.pdf*.

"it was due . . .": Thomas Aquinas, *Commentary on Letter to the Hebrews*, Patristic Bible Commentary, 483, *https://sites.google.com/site/aquinasstudybible/home/hebrews/st-thomas-aquinas-on-hebrews*.

"They did not condemn sacrifices as such": see Charles Hauret, "Sacrifice," trans. Eugene C. Ulrich, in *DBT*, 514.

"salvation will have to arise": *RIM*, 167. The translation is ours. Commentary on Jesus' attitude to sacrifice draws from Behm, "θύω," in *TDNT*, vol. 3, 184.

On the three particular sacrifices of the Old Law fulfilled in Christ, see *TSP*, vol. 2, 182–185; see also *MJC*, 218–220.

Commentary on the Sinai covenant draws from John E. Huesman, "Exodus," in *JBC*, 61; see also *Nav-Pent*, commentary to Ex 24:3–8. "made up of Jew and gentile": Paul VI, *LG*, 9. Commentary on Passover based on "Passover, Feast of," in *CBD*, 679–680.

On the significance of blood in Passover sacrifice, see Huesman, "Exodus," 52.

Regarding the paramount importance of the sacrifice of the lamb, see *WIR*, 144.

Commentary on Lamb based on "Lamb," in *CBD*, 522. "Jesus appears here": *Ratzinger-HW*, 224.

On the Day of Atonement, see *The Oxford Dictionary of the Jewish Religion*, 2nd ed, online edition, ed. Adele Berlin, s.v. "Yom Kippur," *https://doi.org/10.1093/acref/9780199730049.001.0001*.

"He would then invoke the holy name of Yahweh": see *CCC*, 433.

On the expiation of sins through the invocation of the name of Yahweh, see Faley, "Leviticus," in *JBC*, vol. 1, 77.

With regard to the transmission of sins to the goat, the comparison of the Day of Atonement sacrifice with the sacrifice of the covenant, and blood as a "positive symbol," see *WIR*, 141.

Regarding Christ's sacrifice as bringing "*all* of the sacrifices of the Old Testament" to fulfillment, see Hauret, "Sacrifice," 514.

"Christ's charity in a mysterious way takes on the sins of mankind . . .": see *RIM*, 194–195. For summary of the Tradition's reflection on the meaning of Christ's death as sacrifice, see *RIM*, 174–175.

"Because Christ has a real human flesh": see the teachings of St. Cyril of Alexandria, commented on in *GV*, 278.

On Christ as priest and victim, see *TSP*, vol. 2, 185.

"a free, personal act of self-giving": Behm, "θύω," 185.

Regarding the holiness of mankind reaching its high point in this self-giving, see *ITC*, III.1.

8C. Christ's Death as Ransom and Redemption

On the distinction between ransom and redemption, see "apolutrósis" and "lutron" in *Strong's Concordance* (Bible Hub), *https://biblehub.com/greek/*.

On the significance of the Greek words for *ransom* and *redemption* and the Hebrew equivalents, as well as ransom in Mk 10:45, see O. Procksch, "λύω κτλ," in *TDNT*, vol. 4, 329–330.

On the use of *redeem* in the New Testament, see also concordance to "ἐξαγοράζω" in *Blue Letter Bible, https://www.blueletterbible.org/*.

"nowhere does Scripture imply that this price is demanded of God": see *TSP*, vol. 2, 193. About offering of Christ as "exchange," see *WIR*, 130.

On God's transcendence with regard to the duty of ransom, see O. Procksch, "λύω κτλ," 333.

"is a free act of God's grace": the same work, 332. Concerning the attempt to reduce Christ's Redemption to "a symbol or myth," see *ITC*, III.30–34.

Regarding the view that some are "predestined to damnation": see *MJC*, 300. See *MJC*, 301, on man's need to freely make the redemption his own.

On salvation by our personal confession of faith in Christ, see commentary on the teaching of St. Augustine in *GV*, 173.

"bears fruit not only of adoration of God": *RH* 10. "have not yet arrived": *LG*, 16.

Chapter 9: Christ's Glorification: The Resurrection and Ascension

Opening quote: John Paul II, *Memory and Identity* (New York, NY: Rizzoli, 2005), 25.

9A. The Burial and Descent of Christ to Hell

On Christ's dead body as united to the divine Person of the Son, see *MJC*, 225; see also *CCC*, 626.

Regarding Aquinas' position that Christ's corpse did not undergo decay, see *ST*, III, q. 51, art. 3. The quote of Scripture is from the *Summa* text.

On the connection between Christ's death and the Passover sacrifice, see Vawter, "The Gospel According to John," in *JBC*, vol. 2, 462–463.

Regarding the detail of no bone being broken in both the Passover lamb and Christ, see *Ratzinger-HW*, 224.

On St. John's reading of blood and water in terms of baptism and the Eucharist, see Vawter, "The Gospel According to John," 462.

Apropos of the burial site of Jesus, see *Nav-NT*, commentary to Mark 15:42–47. "just when it seems": *Ratzinger-HW*, 228.

On the meaning of the Hebrew *sheol*, see *RIM*, 203.

On Christ's descent to the dead to free the just who awaited him, see *CCC*, 633.

On the descent to hell as showing Christ's desire to bring salvation to all, see *RIM*, 207.

9B. The Event of the Resurrection

On resurrection in distinction from immortality of soul, see N. T. Wright, *The Resurrection of the Son of God* (Minneapolis: Fortress Press, 2003), 82–83.

Regarding the resurrection miracles carried out by Elijah and Elisha, see Jean Radermakers and Pierre Grelot, "Resurrection," in *DBT*, 495.

On the development of OT belief in "concrete bodily resurrection," see Wright, *Resurrection*, 109.

Regarding Ez 37, see Faculty of Theology of the University of Navarre, *Major Prophets*, commentary on Ez 37:1–14.

On the OT vision of the resurrection as being far off and disconnected from the messiah, see Wright, *Resurrection*, 205.

With regard to the resurrection as "much more of a central theme in the New Testament," see Wright, *Resurrection*, 274.

On the impossibility of the Resurrection being "purely a 'spiritual' event," see *MJC*, 237.

Regarding Christ's rising to "a fuller and more perfect form of life," see *RIM*, 213.

On Our Lady as first witness to the Resurrection, see for example Josemaría Escrivá, *Holy Rosary* (London: Scepter, 1987), meditation on the first glorious mystery, *https://www.escrivaworks.org/book/-point-11.htm*.

"as woman was the first to taste death": Bede, *In Marci Evangelium*, 4, 16, 9–10.

Text cited in *Nav-NT*, commentary on Lk 24:1–12.

On the witnesses who establish truth of the Resurrection at the historical level, see *CCC*, 643.

The section on the meaning of the Resurrection through faith draws from *RIM*, 217–218.

On the Church gradually finding a language for the Resurrection in the Scriptures, see Radermakers, "Resurrection," 496.

Analysis of Resurrection passages in the Gospels draws from the following pages of Wright, *Resurrection*: Mk, 628; Mt, 633–635, 643; Lk, 649, 657–660; Jn, 669–673.

Analysis of the OT scriptural context of Christ's resurrection draws from Radermakers, "Resurrection," 497.

9C. The Glorification of Christ as a Result of His Passion

On the Resurrection as an essential part of the Redemption, see *MJC*, 230. This work in turn cites Scheeben, *The Mysteries of Christianity* (St. Louis, MO: Herder, 1946), 436. Analysis of the connection of the Passion and the Resurrection draws from *MJC*, 230–232.

On "new life" as referring to both the life of grace and future resurrection, see *ST*, III, q. 56, art. 2. See also commentary in *RIM*, 222–223.

On Resurrection as "the beginning of a renewed world," see *RIM*, 227.

Concerning the risen Christ as no longer subject to space and time, see *CCC*, 645.

Regarding Christ's humanity as fully taken up into God, see *GHC*, 55. "becomes the representation": *GHC*, 56. Subsequent commentary on love draws from this text.

On the Resurrection as "something essential for our salvation," see *RIM*, 219.

In regard to the risen Christ being free of sin and death, see *RIM*, 229.

On the Resurrection compared to the mustard seed, see *Ratzinger-HW*, 247.

"a new possibility of human existence": *Ratzinger-HW*, 244.

On the absence of hope in the Resurrection narratives and its significance, see Wright, *Resurrection*, 602, 610.

With regard to the mystical significance of immersion of water in baptism, see *TSP*, 210.

On the metaphor of resurrection depending on literal resurrection, see Wright, *Resurrection*, 253.

9D. The Ascension

For analysis of Christ's state after the Resurrection and before ascending into heaven, see *RIM*, 233.

On the complete entrance into an exalted state with the Ascension, see Radermakers, "Resurrection," in *DBT*, 497.

Regarding *raising* in biblical language, see Pierre Benoit, "Ascension," trans. Patrick J. Boyle, in *DBT*, 33.

"the Ascension simply *manifests*": see *MJC*, 248. "the Ascension involves an *exaltation*": see *RIM*, 232, 234.

On the Ascension as revealing meaning of Christ's earthly life, see Radermakers, "Resurrection," 497.

"Christ opens up the path": see *ST*, III, q. 57, art. 6.

Regarding commentary on the kingly figure in Psalm 110, see Roland E. Murphy, "Psalms," in *JBC*, vol. 1, 596.

On the new mode of salvific mediation of Christ after the Ascension, see *RIM*, 236.

9E. The Exaltation of Christ and the Redemptive Meaning of Suffering

On "true and definitive suffering for man," see John Paul II, Apostolic Letter On the Christian Meaning of Human Suffering *Salvifici Doloris* (February 11, 1984), 14, Vatican website: *www.vatican.va*.

With regard to the great pain of damnation as exclusion from communion with God, see *CCC*, 1033.

On the heresies which denied the real body and true suffering of Christ, see *MJC*, 294.

With regard to God's immunity from suffering, see *ST*, III, q. 46, art. 7.

On God as subject of suffering, see *MJC*, 297.

Commentary on the meaning of Christ's suffering and the redemptive suffering of the Christian is based on *Salvifici Doloris*, 17–18, 23.

"an incomparable depth": same document, 17.

See also same document, 22, on how Christ transforms human suffering.

"an invitation to manifest": *Salvifici Doloris*, 22.

"follow in the footsteps . . .": Josemaría Escrivá, *The Way of the Cross* (New York: Scepter, 1990), commentary on Station 14, *https://www.escrivaworks.org/book/the_way_of_the_cross-point-14.htm*.

Chapter 10: The Lordship of Christ

Opening quote: from St. Thérèse of Lisieux, *Story of a Soul. The Autobiography of St. Thérèse of Lisieux*, 3rd ed., trans. John Clarke (Washington, DC: ICS Publications, 1996), 258.

10A. Redemption in Christ and the Sending of the Holy Spirit

"The gift made by the Son": John Paul II, Encyclical Letter On the Holy Spirit in the Life of the Church and the World *Dominum et Vivificantem* (May 18, 1986), 23, Vatican website: *www.vatican.va*. "new beginning": same document, 14.

On connection between the descent of the Holy Spirit upon Our Lady and the descent at Pentecost, see *RIM*, 245.

Commentary on the Jewish feast of Pentecost draws from *Nav-Pent*, commentary on Lv 23:9–14 and Lv 23:15–22.

Regarding Pentecost as the "fruit" of Christ's death, see same work, commentary on Lv 23:15–22.

"the Spirit would become the possession of all": see *GHC*, 121.

On the original sense of Pentecost in reference to the entire Easter season, see Jean Daniélou, *The Bible and the Liturgy* (Notre Dame, IN: University of Notre Dame Press, 1956, reprint ed. 2014), 319.

Quotes from St. Josemaría's feast for Pentecost: *CIPB*, 127.

On Rom 8:11 and the transformation of the body by the Holy Spirit, see Joseph A. Fitzmyer, "The Letter to the Romans," in *JBC*, vol. 2, 315.

On the Holy Spirit's continual work in the mission of Christ and bringing redemption to the human person, see John Paul II, *Dominum et Vivificantem*, 24.

10B. God's Saving Action in the Church

On significance of *pleroma*, see *MJC*, 252.

Regarding the Church as fulfillment of God's promise to dwell with his people, see María del Pilar Río, "Elementos neotestamentarios para un redescubrimiento de la dimensión eclesial del ser cristiano," *Annales Theologici* 24, no. 1 (2010), 53.

With regard to the gift of tongues as sign of universality, see *RIM*, 263.

Commentary on the wounded side based on Paul Ternant, "Church," trans. Glicerio S. Abad, in *DBT*, 75.

"an extension of Christ . . .": *TSP*, vol. 1, 300.

Commentary on the Mystical Body of Christ draws from *TSP*, vol. 1, 300; see also *TSP*, vol. 2, 258–259, 283–285.

On Augustine's doctrine of the Church as *Christus totus*, see *CCC*, 795. "Embracing the Christian faith . . .": *CIPB*, 183. "Christ, the final Adam . . .": *GS*, 22.

"All of these circumstances have a divine meaning through the Incarnation": Commentary on this theme based on *RIM*, 267–268.

"The Church, or, in other words . . .": *LG*, 3.

10C. Redemption as Liberation from Slavery to Sin, to the Devil, and to Death

On the Church's early realization of the liberation from Egypt as figure for Christ's deliverance, see the teaching of Melito of Sardis, described in *GV*, 51.

"it is left for us to wrestle with"; "cannot injure . . .": Council of Trent, *Decree on Original Sin* (June 17, 1546), 5, *https://www.ewtn.com/catholicism/library/decree-concerning-original-sin--decree-concerning-reform-1495*.

"With original sin, man falls prey to the devil": see same decree, 1. Trent here cites Heb 2:14.

On death as source of "anxiety and sadness," see *GS*, 18. "Christians are freed from the *fear of death*": see *MJC*, 263.

With regard to death as a moment for "final glorification," see *MJC*, 264.

"love is the key to freedom": Jutta Burggraf, *Made for Freedom. Loving, Defending, and Living God's Gift* (New Rochelle, NY: Scepter, 2012), 54; subsequent commentary on love draws from this text. For commentary on "Theology of Liberation," see *CDF, Instruction on Certain Aspects of the "Theology of Liberation,"* (August 6, 1984), chap. 9.

"examining his heart . . .": *GS*, 13. Subsequent commentary on disorder of sin draws from this text.

"an authentic faith": Pope Francis, Apostolic Exhortation On the Proclamation of the Gospel in Today's World *Evangelii Gaudium* (November 24, 2013), 183, Vatican website: *www.vatican.va.* "Christ's love and freedom . . .": Josemaría Escrivá, *Furrow* (New York: Scepter, 1987), 302, *https://www.escrivaworks.org/book/furrow-point-302.htm.*

10C. The Second Coming of Christ

"*fortiter et suaviter*": Wisdom 8:1; Latin Vulgate translation, Internet Sacred Text Archive (Evinity Publishing Inc., 2020), *https://www.sacredtexts.com/bib/vul/wis008.htm.*

On *Parousia* as indicating a solemn arrival, see Albrecht Oepke, "παρουσία, πάρειμι" in *TDNT*, vol. 5, 859. See also *MJC*, 254.

"The description draws from the Old Testament": McKenzie, "The Gospel According to Matthew," in *JBC*, vol. 2, 105.

Concerning *Parousia* as conclusion of the history of salvation, see *RIM*, 310. "in the presence of Christ": *CCC* here makes reference to Jn 12:49.

"The deeper divine meaning . . ." see *CCC*, 1040.

On "*Day of the Lord*" in the Old Testament, see Paul Auvray and Xavier Léon-Dufour, "Day of the Lord," trans. Maurice J. Moore, in *DBT*, 111.

"In the present life . . .": see *GS*, 24.

The description of the renewal of man and the entire universe, with the Second Coming, draws in particular from *RIM*, 310–311.

On the "incomplete" nature of the kingdom of God in history, see *LG*, 5.

ACKNOWLEDGMENTS

In this work I am obviously grateful for the many theologians who have developed the rich topic of soteriology, whose profound insights I have sought to transmit. In particular I am thankful to my own teacher of this subject, Professor Antonio Ducay of the Pontifical University of the Holy Cross. Gratitude is also a due to Larry Olsen and those who have reviewed this text. Thanks additionally go to the entire team at Scepter Publishers, especially Robert Singerline and Meredith Koopman, for their diligent work at the service of Catholic publishing. Finally, I would also like to mention my family and especially my parents, George and Mariamma Thomas, who have supported me along my educational journey. As long as that journey has taken, a project like this reminds me that our learning never comes to an end . . .